Lecture Notes in Computer Science 2169
Edited by G. Goos, J. Hartmanis, and J. van Leeuwen

Springer

Berlin
Heidelberg
New York
Barcelona
Hong Kong
London
Milan
Paris
Tokyo

Michael Jaedicke

New Concepts for Parallel Object-Relational Query Processing

Springer

Series Editors

Gerhard Goos, Karlsruhe University, Germany
Juris Hartmanis, Cornell University, NY, USA
Jan van Leeuwen, Utrecht University, The Netherlands

Author

Michael Jaedicke
Donnersbergerstr. 34
80634 München
Germany
E-mail: mjaedicke@yahoo.com

Cataloging-in-Publication Data applied for

Die Deutsche Bibliothek - CIP-Einheitsaufnahme

Jaedicke, Michael: New concepts for parallel object relational query processing /
Michael Jaedicke. - Berlin ; Heidelberg ; New York ; Barcelona ;
Hong Kong ; London ; Milan ; Paris ; Tokyo : Springer, 2001
    (Lecture notes in computer science ; Vol. 2169)
    Zugl.: Stuttgart, Univ., Diss., 1999
    ISBN 978-3-540-42781-0

CR Subject Classification (1998): E.2, H.2

ISSN 0302-9743
ISBN 978-3-540-42781-0 Springer-Verlag Berlin Heidelberg New York

Springer-Verlag Berlin Heidelberg New York
a member of BertelsmannSpringer Science+Business Media GmbH

http://www.springer.de

© Springer-Verlag Berlin Heidelberg 2001

Typesetting: Camera-ready by author, data conversion by Christian Grosche, Hamburg
Printed on acid-free paper   SPIN: 10840389   06/3142   5 4 3 2 1 0

Preface

When I started this research, no commercial database system supported both object-relational features and parallelism. In the meantime this situation has changed dramatically. All major vendors now offer a parallel, object-relational DBMS as their high-end product. However, there is still a lot to do. Firstly, object-relational (or extensible) DBMS have yet to mature fully. Secondly, the integration of parallelism and extensibility has not yet been completed. This work is my attempt to make a contribution to both issues.

Some of the concepts and techniques developed have been implemented in a prototypical parallel database system called MIDAS. This system is the result of a team effort to which many people have contributed. My own contributions to the system are the user-defined functions and user-defined table operators, the extension of the system tables for those user-defined objects and for detailed statistics, and the new query optimizer, for which I worked with Clara Nippl. She contributed especially to the cost model, the physical operators, and implementation rules. Furthermore, I provided support for the development of concepts for the query parallelizer, the query execution control system, and the send/receive operators of the execution system.

Acknowledgments

I am very thankful to Professor Dr.-Ing. habil. Bernhard Mitschang, who gave me the opportunity to carry out this research. His continuous support, encouragement, and useful comments during many fruitful discussions and during the preparation of joint publications are especially acknowledged.

I am very grateful to Prof. Dr.-Ing. Theo Härder who introduced me thoroughly to database systems and taught me a lot about engineering. I am also grateful to him for the analysis of my results and his valuable remarks.

I also acknowledge the help of my colleagues Giannis Bozas, Clara Nippl, Angelika Reiser, and Stephan Zimmermann with whom I worked together on the MIDAS project. Stephan provided software engineering support for the whole group and was always helpful. His work centered on PVM communication, the process architecture, buffer and transaction management, the parallelization of the execution system, the scheduler and benchmarking, and performance. Clara worked on the parallelization of the execution system, the scheduler, the parallelizer, and the optimizer. Giannis focussed on the lock manager and the buffer management. I also thank Prof. Rudolf Bayer, who led the project together with Prof. Mitschang, for his support.

I also enjoyed giving practical courses on RDBMS together with Angelika. I thank all my colleagues in Munich and Stuttgart, especially Aiko Frank, Volker Markl, Jürgen Sellentin, and Martin Zirkel for their help and comradeship during the last years. I am grateful to my colleague Ralf Rantzau and to Prof. Härder for improving my English.

Special thanks also go to the students that I have supervised: Pascal Frantz, Stefan Haas, Karl Hahn, Sebastian Heupel, Bernd Holzhey, Kay Krueger-Barvels, Sabine Perathoner, Ralf Schumacher, Robert Seehafer, and Susanne Stamp. It was a pleasure to work with them. Many of them made significant contributions to this work. I also thank the many other students who worked on the MIDAS project.

I also gratefully acknowledge the valuable comments of the anonymous referees of diverse papers, which have also improved this work. The feedback from C. Mohan, G. Lohman, and M. Carey on the issue of interfaces for query execution plans and the feedback from Harald Schöning on the parallel execution of user-defined functions is much appreciated.

Finally, I would like to thank the Deutsche Forschungsgemeinschaft (DFG) for funding the MIDAS project (SFB 342, B2). I also acknowledge the support of the Studienstiftung des Deutschen Volkes during my university course.

Special thanks go to Springer-Verlag, especially to Alfred Hofmann, and the series editors, for publishing my work in LNCS.

Last but not least I am grateful to my parents for their affection and continuous care.

July 2001   Michael Jaedicke

Abstract

During the last few years parallel object-relational database management systems have emerged as the leading data management technology on the market place. These systems are extensible by user-defined data types and user-defined functionality for the data. This work focuses on the efficient parallel execution of user-defined functionality. The main contributions describe techniques to support data parallelism for user-defined scalar and aggregate functions, to support intra-function parallelism for the execution of a scalar function on a large object, and a new technology to provide extensibility with regard to new set-oriented database operations that can efficiently implement user-defined functionality in parallel object-relational database management systems. Some of these techniques have been implemented in the MIDAS prototype or on top of a commercial object-relational database management system.

Table of Contents

CHAPTER 8   *Summary, Conclusions, and Future Work*

References

Appendix A

CHAPTER 1

Introduction

1.1 ORDBMS: The Next Great Wave

During the last few years, it became obvious that object-relational database management systems (ORDBMS) are the next great wave in database technology ([15], [96],
[104]). ORDBMS have been proposed for all data intensive applications that need
both complex queries and complex data types [104]. Typical ORDBMS application
areas are e.g. multi-media [70] and image applications [77], especially for web databases [58], geographic information systems ([89], [107]), and management of time
series [6] and documents [52]. Many of these applications pose high requirements
with respect to functionality and performance on ORDBMS. Since the data volumes
that come along with new data types like satellite images, videos, CAD objects, etc.
are gigantic and the queries are complex, parallel database technology is essential for
many of these applications. These observations have in recent years led to significant
development efforts for parallel ORDBMS (PORDBMS) of some database vendors
([19], [81], [83], [85]). Although first industrial implementations enter the marketplace and the SQL3 standard [69] is maturing, there are still many topics left for
research in this area ([13], [23], [24], [85], [98]).

One of the current goals for ORDBMS is to move towards a framework for constructing parallel ADT [13] and more sophisticated query optimization and execution
([13], [98]). User-defined functions (UDF) are completely opaque for query optimizers and thus allow only very restricted query optimization and execution techniques,
if no further optimization and execution information is provided. Additional information enables more sophisticated query optimization and execution as the
ORDBMS knows and understands at least part of the semantics of the ADT. This
results in great performance improvements ([98], [104]). While there are different
approaches to reach this goal ([13], [98], [104]), most ORDBMS vendors currently
offer ADT developers only a few parameters to describe the semantics of user-
defined functions. This is by far not sufficient.

In this work, we make several contributions to query processing in PORDBMS.
First, we have proposed techniques to support parallel execution for a broad class of

M. Jaedicke: Parallel Object-Relational Query Processing, LNCS 2169, pp. 1-4, 2001.

user-defined functions. This includes not only techniques for the traditional parallel execution based on data parallelism, but also methods that support intra-function parallelism. The latter is useful, when a single, expensive function is evaluated on a large object (LOB).

Second, we have proposed two approaches to enhance query execution plans with user-defined functions by means of semantic information. One approach allows developers to manipulate query execution plans directly. The other approach allows developers to extend the query optimizer so that it has more alternatives for the implementation of a user-defined function. This method can also be used to provide a convenient invocation of complex operations in SQL statements, i.e., as a 'macro' concept for SQL.

Third, we have designed and implemented a method to extend the compiler and the database engine by new application-specific database operators. The main concept is here the invention of a generic database operator, whose functionality can be programmed by developers.

Before we start with the main topics, we briefly review some aspects of the historic development of extensible DBMS in subsection 1.2 and present an overview over this work in subsection 1.3.

1.2 Extensible DBMS

The idea to develop extensible DBMS has been around for a while now. During the last fifteen years, the concept of extensible DBMS matured considerably. In the early times of extensible DBMS, with prototypes like POSTGRES [108], STARBURST [37] and EXODUS [14], two different directions evolved: on the one hand, the focus was on constructing DBMS that could be easily extended by the DBMS vendors themselves. The goal of this line of research was to construct specialized DBMS with extensions for certain application domains. The other direction of extensibility is best described as DBMS customizing and corresponds to the view of the current commercial ORDBMS technology. In this view DBMS vendors build complete systems that have a generic or universal character. That is, the DBMS has a set of interfaces that allows to register external programs together with information on their appropriate use within the DBMS. This allows third-party vendors like independent software vendors (ISVs) to build *packages* that extend the DBMS functionality for some application domain (there are package standardization efforts for some application domains in SQL/MM [101]). Furthermore, it is possible to combine several of these packages. This allows to support a broad range of applications with a single system. DBMS vendors have different names for their packages like DataBlades, Extenders, Cartridges, or Snap-Ins.

The core technology of current ORDBMS consists of a set of generic components. These components can invoke external routines that have been registered before and they can use information from the system tables. As a result, they are highly flexible and can be used to customize the DBMS functionality. Examples of such components are rule- and cost-based query optimizers, generic index structures, generic storage structures (LOBs), and database operators that can invoke user-defined routines.

1.3 Overview

We give here an overview over the following chapters. The second chapter provides the necessary *background*. We restrict ourselves to the concepts of direct relevance for this work.

Chapter 3 considers the *parallel execution of UDF*. In this chapter, we develop techniques that allow to process user-defined scalar and aggregate functions with data parallelism. We describe the class of partitionable functions that can be processed in parallel. We also propose an extension which allows to speed up processing of another large class of functions by means of parallel sorting. Functions that can be processed by means of our techniques are often used in decision support queries on large data volumes, for example. Hence, a parallel execution is indispensable.

In Chapter 4 we propose an approach to *intra-function parallelism*, which has the goal to support parallel processing of an expensive function on a single large object. This kind of parallelism is important, because many object-relational extensions support expensive functions on large data objects. One important application of large objects is the processing of digital images as for example generated by digital cameras. Intra-function parallelism is orthogonal to data parallelism and to our knowledge is not yet exploited in any PORDBMS. Our approach is to extend the execution system of a PORDBMS by means of two new operators: decompose and compose. The decompose operator breaks a large object into pieces and the compose operator assembles a large object from these pieces. As we show, these operators can be implemented efficiently by means of descriptors for large objects. We present an initial performance evaluation using an implementation on top of a PORDBMS that demonstrates the effect of the new operators. As our measurements indicate, a good speedup can be achieved.

Chapter 5 introduces the *multi-operator method* for the implementation of specific algorithms for user-defined join predicates that take the predicate semantics into account. There has been a long record of research for efficient join algorithms in RDBMS, but user-defined join predicates in ORDBMS are typically evaluated using a restriction after forming the complete Cartesian product. While there has been some research on join algorithms for non-traditional data (e.g. spatial joins), today's ORDBMS offer developers no general mechanism that allows to implement user-defined join predicates in an efficient way. We propose the multi-operator method to achieve this goal and show that it is suitable to implement joins with complex user-defined predicates much more efficiently than today. Our approach fits well into the architectural framework of current PORDBMS. A further significant benefit is that the multi-operator method, in our view, can serve as an enabling technique for the parallel execution of complex user-defined functions.

Chapter 6 introduces *user-defined table operators*. We view this concept as our main contribution to object-relational query processing. A central enhancement of object-relational database technology is the possibility to execute arbitrary user-defined functions within SQL statements. We show the limits of this approach and propose user-defined table operators as a new concept that allows the definition and implementation of arbitrary new N-ary database operators, which can be programmed using SQL or embedded SQL (with some extensions). Our approach leads to a new dimension of extensibility that allows to push more application code into the server with full support for efficient and parallel processing. We present and discuss some example applications of user-defined table operators that demonstrate their benefits. Furthermore, user-defined table operators allow performance enhancements of orders of magnitude for the evaluation of various classes of queries with complex user-defined functions. While our approach fits well into the architectures of current commercial object-relational database management systems, it affects nevertheless many DBMS components.

Chapter 7 presents the *implementation of user-defined table operators* in the PORDBMS prototype MIDAS. We show the necessary extensions of the SQL compiler, the optimizer, the parallelizer, the database engine and transaction management and give a brief evaluation. We also discuss further optimization issues for the execution of UDTO.

Chapter 8 contains a summary of this work, our conclusions, and our suggestions for future work. Appendix A provides some additional material.

CHAPTER 2

Background on User-Defined Routines

We now briefly present the basic concepts and definitions that we use in this work. We refer the reader to the literature for the general concepts of parallel relational ([4], [22], [29], [41], [73], [103], [110]) and object-relational query processing ([13], [15], [17], [20], [40], [45], [47], [102], [104]).

2.1 User-Defined Routines

Every RDBMS comes with a fixed set of built-in functions. These functions can be either scalar functions or aggregate functions. The latter are also called set or column functions. A *scalar function* can be used in SQL queries wherever an expression can be used. Typical scalar functions are arithmetic functions like + and * or concat for string concatenation. Functions for type casting are special scalar functions, too. A scalar function is applied to the values of a row of an input table.

By contrast, an *aggregate function* is applied to the values of a single column of either a group of rows or of all rows of an input table. A group of rows occurs if a GROUP-BY clause is used. Thus, aggregate functions can be used in the projection part of SQL queries and in HAVING clauses. The aggregate functions of the SQL-92 standard are MAX, MIN, AVG, SUM and COUNT. Other statistical aggregate functions like standard deviation and variance are provided by some RDBMS implementations, e.g. [15].

In ORDBMS it is possible to use a *user-defined function* (**UDF**) at nearly all places where a system-provided built-in function can appear in SQL-92. Thus, there are two subsets of UDF: *user-defined scalar functions* (**UDSF**) and *user-defined aggregate functions* (**UDAF**). A UDSF that returns a boolean value is also called *user-defined predicate* (**UDP**). Finally, some ORDBMS (e.g. [50]) offer the possibility to write *user-defined table functions* (**UDTF**), which return a table. UDTF can be referenced exactly in the same way as views or tables in the FROM clause of SELECT statements. We use the term *user-defined routines* (**UDR**) as a generic term for all user-

M. Jaedicke: Parallel Object-Relational Query Processing, LNCS 2169, pp. 5-13, 2001.

defined procedural extensions of DBMS. With the term *routines* we denote both, user-defined procedural extensions and built-in (or system-generated) functions.

ORDBMS need an extensible parser, an extensible optimizer, an extensible executor (or engine), an extensible index and storage manager and extensible utilities to be able to handle statements which contain UDR. All extensible components need metadata to deal with UDR correctly. Often metadata is also useful to improve the efficiency of the execution. This metadata is stored in the system tables as usual. For UDR, important kinds of metadata are: the signature, the description of its implementation, auxiliary functions for cost and selectivity estimation, and options for optimization or execution. This metadata is provided by developers when they create new UDR. We will discuss the details in the next section.

2.2 Definition, Implementation, and Execution of New UDR

We now briefly describe how UDR are created in ORDBMS. The creation of a new UDR consists of two steps: First, an implementation for the UDR must be provided. Second, the UDR must be registered with the DBMS. During this registration the needed metadata must be provided, too.

Developers can implement a UDR either as a so-called *external* UDR or reuse the implementation of an already existing routine (*sourced* UDR). Sourced UDR are primarily of interest in connection with *user-defined distinct types* (UDTs). UDTs are created as a new type, but they share their representation with a built-in data type like INTEGER. This built-in data type is called *source type*. They have been introduced to support application-specific domains by means of strong typing. Sourced UDR simply allow to transfer UDR of a source type to its UDTs. Because a sourced UDR is directly derived from an existing routine, it is handled exactly as this routine during the compilation, optimization and execution of queries. Hence, we do not deal with sourced UDR in the remainder of this work and concentrate on external UDR.

An external UDR is implemented as a function in a third-generation programming language (typically C, C++ and Java are supported as languages). This function is compiled into a dynamic link library (DLL), which can be linked to a process at run-time. The DBMS needs only access to the DLL to execute the function. Therefore, developers do not have to ship the source code along with the package that contains the UDR. This has the advantage that the implementation of the UDR is not disclosed, which is often a requirement of independent software vendors. On the other hand, the implementation is opaque for the DBMS, i.e., the UDR is a black-box. For this reason, the DBMS cannot reasonably try to analyze the implementation of a UDR in order to obtain information for query optimization and execution.

Another important aspect of external functions is that they may be a threat for DBMS reliability and security, because it is desirable to execute the UDR directly within the DBMS kernel process. In this case, the UDR is executed with all privileges. That is, it can access and modify all data in the database as well as internal data structures of the DBMS. Moreover, errors in the UDR can bring down the entire DBMS. Hence, vendors have created the possibility to use sand-boxing techniques in order to make the execution of UDR safe. One such technique is to execute a UDR in a different less privileged process. Another technique is to code the UDR in Java and to integrate a Java virtual machine directly into the DBMS kernel. Because Java allows only restricted access to system resources this results in safe UDR. However, all sand-boxing techniques can aggravate performance. For example, if an additional process is used then the parameters of the UDR must be passed via inter-process communication. Therefore, some vendors also offer quality control and certification programs for independent software vendors that develop packages. Certified packages should be safe and are allowed to run directly within the DBMS kernel.

UDR are not limited with regard to the effect of their actions. UDR can perform *external actions*, e.g. read from or write to a file, send an email to the database administrator, start a program, etc. Moreover, the Informix Illustra ORDBMS supports UDF that consist of one or more SQL statements. However, these SQL statements cannot be embedded into procedural code. We say that such a UDR performs *database actions*. A UDR that performs external or database actions has an *external context*.

So far the description holds for all kinds of UDR. In the following subsections, we provide more details for the different kinds of UDR. We also describe the corresponding metadata and its usage.

2.2.1   User-Defined Scalar Functions

Figure 1 provides an example of the syntax of the CREATE FUNCTION statement that is used in DB2 UDB [15] to register a new UDSF with the DBMS. The scalar function add returns the sum of its two arguments of the UDT dollar. It is created as an external function in the example, but we could have derived it also from a corresponding function of the source type of dollar.
As can be seen from this example, some options provide metadata that describe the characteristics of the registered function. We discuss these options briefly and refer the reader to [15] for further details. First, the name of the UDSF and its signature are specified. The clause EXTERNAL NAME provides the name of the DLL and the name of the function within this library that serves as implementation. Then, the developer has specified that the C programming language was used for the implementation. PARAMETER STYLE DB2SQL specifies the way in which the DBMS passes the parameters to the UDSF. The option NOT VARIANT tells the DBMS that the UDSF has a deterministic behavior. The UDSF can be executed directly within the DBMS kernel process, because the option NOT FENCED is specified. Otherwise

```
CREATE FUNCTION add (dollar, dollar)
RETURNS dollar
EXTERNAL NAME 'dollar!add'
LANGUAGE C
PARAMETER STYLE DB2SQL
NOT VARIANT
NOT FENCED
NOT NULL CALL
NO SQL
NO EXTERNAL ACTION
NO SCRATCHPAD
NO FINAL CALL;
```

Figure 1. Registration of a New UDSF add in DB2.

the function is executed within a process that runs under a special user ID which is determined by the database administrator. NOT NULL CALL specifies that the result of the function is NULL, if one or more of its arguments are NULL. In this case the function is not invoked. This option can be used to avoid the handling of NULL values in the implementation, if this is not needed. This function does neither perform database actions (NO SQL) nor external actions (NO EXTERNAL ACTION). Database actions are currently not supported in DB2.

The last two options tell the DBMS that the UDSF does not use a so-called SCRATCHPAD. A scratchpad area is a small piece of memory that is passed to a UDSF with all calls and that is not deleted after the executed function returns the control. This allows to preserve information from one function invocation to the next. Thus, it is possible for a function to maintain a global context (or global state). After the last call to the function within an SQL statement, the scratchpad is deallocated by the system. However before this happens, there is an optional FINAL CALL to the function that can be used to clean up resources that were allocated by the function. For example, developers can allocate more memory than the rather small scratchpad area by dynamically allocating a piece of memory and hooking it up in the scratchpad. Often a scratchpad is used to store intermediate results that have been computed from the arguments of former function calls. We say that such UDSF have an *input context*. A simple example of a UDSF with a scratchpad is a function sequence_no that returns the number of its invocations so far.

After the function has been registered with DB2, the developer should provide the query optimizer some information about the expected execution costs of this UDSF. ORDBMS have to provide a suitable interface for this. In general, a user-defined cost estimation function could be provided. However, for UDSF the costs will typically be estimated as a simple combination of several parameters. Therefore a simpler interface is usually considered as sufficient. For example, DB2 UDB [15] allows to specify the I/O and CPU costs that are expected for the first call to a function, for each further call, and per argument byte that is read by the function. In addition to this, the percentage of the argument's storage size that is processed at the average call to the UDF should be specified. The costs that are related to the size of arguments are primarily of interest for UDSF which operate on LOB data, since the size of the arguments (and therefore the cost of the function) can vary by several orders of magnitude. Based on this information and the estimated number of invocations the DBMS computes the estimated costs. If a UDSF returns a boolean value the developer should be able to specify a user-defined selectivity estimation function [104]. This is helpful for the case that the UDSF is used as a predicate in the WHERE or HAVING clause. However, if the UDSF is used within an expression, it is necessary to estimate the value distribution of the UDSF results. We are not aware of support for this in current commercial ORDBMS or research prototypes. In general, providing these details for cost and selectivity estimation can be a time-consuming task. Hence, easy to use graphical environments are offered for the development of UDF ([19], [55], [81]).

2.2.2   User-Defined Aggregate Functions

UDAF are applied to a set of values that corresponds to the values of an entire column of a table. The execution of UDAF is well integrated into the usual one-tuple-at-a-time processing style of the engine. Hence, they are not called once with all values of a column as an argument, but instead they are called once for each value of the column. This results into two requirements: First, there must be an appropriate interface for developers that is tailored to this style of processing and second, there is the need to preserve the intermediate result from one invocation to the next.

Let us now see how the Informix Illustra ORDBMS [53] supports UDAF, for example. The system computes aggregate functions one-tuple-at-a-time, i.e., there is one function call for each element of the argument set. The user has to write the three following external functions to implement a new UDAF:

- *Init*():
    The Init function is called only once and without arguments to initialize the aggregate computation before the actual computation of the aggregate begins. It returns a pointer to a memory area, which it has allocated to store intermediate results during the aggregation.
- *Iter*(pointer, value):
    The Iter function is called once for each element of the input set. One parameter passes the value of the input element and the other passes the pointer to the allocated memory area. It aggregates the next value into the current aggregate that is stored using the pointer. It returns the pointer to the allocated memory area.
- aggregate value = *Final*(pointer):
    The Final function is called once after the last element of the input set has been

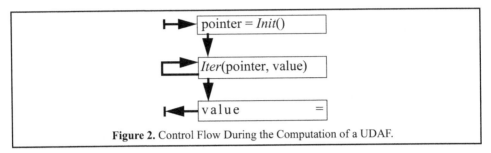

Figure 2. Control Flow During the Computation of a UDAF.

processed by the Iter function. It computes and returns the resulting aggregate using the pointer to the allocated memory area. In addition, it deallocates the memory.

The control flow during the aggregate computation is presented in Figure 2. The pointer, similar to the scratchpad area mentioned in subsection 2.2.1, allows to store the input context of the computation. For example to compute the average of a set of values, the *Iter* function would store both the sum of all values seen so far and their number as intermediate results in the allocated memory area. The *Final* function would divide the sum by the number and return the result. The reader should note that all practical aggregate functions have an input context.

Obviously this design matches the usual Open-Next-Close protocol ([29], [73]) for relational operators. After the three functions have been registered with the ORDBMS (cf. Figure 1), the user can create the aggregate function (e.g. average) using a CREATE AGGREGATE statement. This statement specifies the three functions that implement the *Init, Iter* and *Final* functions for the new aggregate function.

2.2.3   User-Defined Table Functions

A UDTF is invoked with some scalar arguments and returns a table. In DB2 UDB, a UDTF together with its arguments can only be referenced in the FROM clause of a SELECT statement [50]. It can be referenced in exactly the same way as a table or view. The purpose of a table function is typically to access external data that is not stored in the database, convert it dynamically into a table and make it available within a SELECT statement. Examples are the access to emails that are stored in a file or the access to a collection of World Wide Web pages.

A difference to references of base tables or views is that one can also use correlated table functions. In this case an argument of the UDTF is the attribute of a row. The reference to the corresponding table T must be either in a higher-level of the hierarchy of subqueries or in the same FROM clause left to the reference of the UDTF. Such a correlated UDTF is not evaluated once. Rather it is evaluated once for each row r of the table T and produces result tables E(r). The result of a reference to the table T and the correlated UDTF is then the union of the Cartesian products between a row of T and the corresponding result table E(r), i.e.:

$$\bigcup_{r \in T} \{ \{r\} \times E(r) \}. \qquad \text{(EQ 1)}$$

There are roughly the same options for the registration of UDTF as for UDSF. However, one important exception holds. The optimizer has no way to estimate the cardinality of the result table of the UDTF. Therefore it should be possible to provide a user-defined cardinality estimation function. However, in practice, a constant value that provides the expected average cardinality might be sufficient. For example, this scheme is used in DB2 UDB.

In DB2 UDB, UDTF are implemented and executed similar to UDSF. Although a table function delivers a table, the interface between the DBMS kernel and the UDTF is one-tuple-at-a-time. To support the return of multiple rows, there are three types of calls available: OPEN, FETCH and CLOSE. A special parameter indicates the type of call to the UDTF. The first call to a UDTF is the OPEN call. For this call all argument values are passed. This call serves to do all initializations (e.g. of a scratchpad), but no result tuple should be returned. Then the DBMS makes as many FETCH calls to the UDTF, until the table function returns the end-of-table condition in the SQLSTATE parameter. With each FETCH call the same argument values as in the OPEN call are passed. After the last tuple has been fetched, the DBMS makes a final CLOSE call. No argument values are passed with this CLOSE call and no tuple should be returned. It serves to release system resources acquired during the OPEN and FETCH calls.

The reader may have already noticed that similar techniques are used for the execution of UDSF with a scratchpad, UDAF, and UDTF. In all cases, a set of rows is processed as input to or output from a UDR. Hence, a technique to integrate the passing of sets with the usual one-tuple-at-a-time processing has to be made available.

2.2.4   User-Defined Functions and Large Objects

In some ORDBMS descriptors (called locators) can be used to manipulate *large objects* (LOBs) in an efficient way ([15], [63]). These locators can also be used as parameters for UDF in order to avoid the passing of the complete LOB as a parameter. A special LOB locator API allows the manipulation of LOBs by means of these locators within the body of an external UDF. For example, there are functions like `length`, `substr`, `append`, `create_locator` and `free_locator` in the API of DB2 UDB [50]. Manipulations of LOBs by means of locators and these functions are first done with the locators. The LOB data in the database is modified only if this is necessary, e.g., if a modified LOB is inserted into a table.

2.3 Comparison with Stored Procedures

In [104] one can find some interesting remarks that give insight into the relationship between UDF and stored procedures in relational systems that we want to cite here:

> ... Basically, a database procedure is a collection of SQL statements with other statements interspersed in a vendor-proprietary programming language. Database procedures were pioneered by Britton-Lee as a performance enhancement for transaction processing applications and subsequently adopted by all major relational vendors. Using traditional SQL, the TPC-C benchmark is five commands that result in 10 messages between client and server processes [31]. With a database procedure defined on the server, the user merely executes it and only two messages are required.

> Note that a database procedure is merely a user-defined function written in a proprietary language that accepts SQL-92 data types as arguments. Unfortunately, the only operation available for database procedures is to execute them. In contrast to user-defined functions they cannot appear in the middle of SQL commands. Thus, they should be considered "brain-dead" user-defined functions. [citation: [104], pp. 33-34]

However, one problem with UDF is that current ORDBMS are still to a large extent "brain-dead" with regard to the optimization and efficient execution of UDF. We will briefly present this optimization problem in the next section. Later, we will present our improvements to this situation.

2.4 Optimization of Queries with UDF

One of the most challenging areas in query processing is query optimization. It is the goal of query optimization to find for a given query a query execution plan (QEP) with very low (or even the lowest possible) costs. The search for a suitable plan is usually constrained by time and space limits. The overall set of query execution plans is determined by the abilities of the database engine. The search space for a given query is the set of all semantically equivalent query execution plans (the equivalence class of a certain query). The size of this equivalence class is determined by the semantic knowledge of the optimizer. In modern rule- and cost-based optimizers ([30], [36], [67]) this semantic knowledge is typically expressed as a set of rules. A cost model is used to estimate the costs of the QEPs. Of course, this cost model and the set of rules contain semantic information.

Obviously, new UDF have also certain semantics that must be made known to the optimizer. Otherwise, the resulting QEP might be incorrect, because certain rules are no longer correct equivalence transformations, or no efficient plan can be found, because the equivalence class of the query is too small. If the cost model is not appropriate, errors in cost estimation might lead to the choice of an actually bad QEP. We have already discussed that developers can influence the cost model by giving constant cost factors for UDF. These cost factors are used to calculate the estimated costs during the optimization.

We remark here that traditional optimizers had to be extended to place predicates with expensive UDF in the best possible way into QEPs [45]. The reason is that traditionally restrictions have been considered as cheap compared to joins. As a result, they were pushed down as far as possible independent of their cost. This approach had to be modified with the introduction of expensive predicates. Chaudhuri and Shim proposed how the well-known optimization approach of System R can be extended appropriately [17].

The central question is, how developers can influence the set of optimization rules. It seems that current systems have only a limited possibility to do this. Obviously, it would be desirable to be able to extend the rule set of the optimizer by arbitrary new rules. This is immediately clear with respect to commutativity and associativity of UDF, since the order of operations can have a huge impact on performance. For example, consider that we want to invert a small part of a digital photo. We can invert the photo and then clip the desired part from the result. However, if we change the order of the operations, then we have to invert only the clipped part of the photo. Naturally, the second execution strategy is by far better [98]. No commercial database system supports extensibility of the optimizer by arbitrary new rules. However, developers can influence the applicability of certain optimization rules by providing appropriate metadata during the registration of UDF. Depending on the properties of a given function some rules are applicable or not. For example, developers must specify for a UDSF, whether this function is deterministic or not. If a function is not deterministic, this function should not be computed several times during the query execution, even if this is cheaper than the materialization of the function's result. The same holds for UDF with external actions, since these actions must normally be executed exactly once.

So far, we have only considered the sequential execution of UDR. In the next chapter, we propose new techniques to parallelize the execution of UDR. We provide the necessary background on parallelism there.

CHAPTER 3

Parallel Processing of User-Defined Functions

3.1 Introduction

Our main contribution in this chapter is to show how a broad class of user-defined functions can be processed in parallel. This class includes both, user-defined scalar functions and user-defined aggregate functions. To this aim we propose a framework covering both the necessary interfaces that allow the appropriate registration of user-defined aggregate functions with the ORDBMS and their parallel processing. Parallel computing of user-defined aggregate functions is especially useful for application domains like decision support (e.g. based on a data warehouse that stores traditional as well as non-traditional data, like spatial, text or image data), as decision support queries often must compute complex aggregates. For example, in the TPC-D Benchmark 15 out of the 17 queries contain aggregate operations [99]. In addition, if scalar functions with a global context are processed in parallel, caution is needed in order to get semantically correct results. Our framework can help in this case, too. Furthermore, we show that some aggregate functions can easily be implemented, if their input is sorted, and they can thus profit from parallel sorting.

We do not consider the parallel execution of table functions due to the following reasons: First, data parallelism cannot be reasonably applied to table functions since a table function is conceptually only invoked once and does not operate on a set. Second, table functions are often used to access external data in practical applications [21], i.e., they perform external actions like reading from a file. This kind of behavior usually inhibits a parallel execution of the body.

The remainder of this chapter is as follows: In section 3.2, we show the limits of user-defined functions with respect to parallel execution. Our framework for parallel processing of user-defined functions is introduced in section 3.3. Section 3.4 presents some examples for the application of the proposed techniques and section 3.5 contains a brief performance analysis. After a discussion of related work in section 3.6, the closing section 3.7 contains a short summary.

M. Jaedicke: Parallel Object-Relational Query Processing, LNCS 2169, pp. 14-32, 2001.
© Springer-Verlag Berlin Heidelberg 2001

3.2 Limits of Current ORDBMS

We will now describe the limits of current ORDBMS with respect to the parallel execution of UDF. To provide a concrete example, we refer to the user-defined aggregate function MOST_FREQUENT, which computes the most frequently occurring integer value in a column of type integer. We have omitted some details (for example the registration parameters, cf. Figure 1) to make the presentation as simple as possible.

We first have to create three UDSF INIT_MF, ITER_MF, FINAL_MF that provide the implementation routines of the MOST_FREQUENT aggregate function. These three routines are programmed as external functions, i.e., they are written e.g. in C and can use the system-provided API for UDF to handle tasks like memory allocation, etc. Then they are registered using the CREATE FUNCTION statement:

```
CREATE FUNCTION INIT_MF()
RETURNS POINTER
EXTERNAL NAME 'libfuncs!mf_init'
LANGUAGE C ...;

CREATE FUNCTION ITER_MF(POINTER, INTEGER)
RETURNS POINTER
EXTERNAL NAME 'libfuncs!mf_iter'
LANGUAGE C ...;

CREATE FUNCTION FINAL_MF()
RETURNS INTEGER
EXTERNAL NAME 'libfuncs!mf_final'
LANGUAGE C ...;
```

The function INIT_MF allocates and initializes memory to store the integer values together with a count and returns a pointer to that memory. The function ITER_MF stores its argument in the allocated memory, if it is an integer value not seen so far, and increments the count for this value. Finally, the FINAL_MF function searches for the value with the maximum count and returns this value. Next, we create the UDAF with the CREATE AGGREGATE statement:

```
CREATE AGGREGATE MOST_FREQUENT
(
init = INIT_MF()
iter = ITER_MF(POINTER, INTEGER)
final = FINAL_MF(POINTER)
);
```

Now the MOST_FREQUENT function can be used as a new aggregate function in queries. We will now explain, why this aggregate function cannot be processed in parallel.

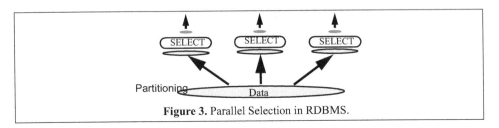

Figure 3. Parallel Selection in RDBMS.

UDSF without context can be executed in parallel using data parallelism. Instead of executing a set of function invocations in a sequential order, one simply partitions the data set (horizontal fragmentation) and processes the UDSF for each data partition in parallel. This parallel execution scheme is shown in Figure 3 for a selection.

Obviously aggregate functions cannot use this approach without modification as they have an input context and deliver only a single result for a set of input tuples. Parallel aggregation operations in RDBMS use an execution scheme consisting of two steps [29] as shown in Figure 4. After the data has been partitioned, it is first aggregated locally for each partition and then, in a second step, the locally computed sub-aggregates are combined in a global aggregation (merging step in Figure 4). For the aggregate function COUNT the local aggregation counts while the global aggregation computes the sum of the local counts. Generally speaking, the local and global aggregation functions needed for parallel execution are different from the aggregate function that is used for sequential execution. For built-in aggregate functions local and global aggregation functions are system-provided. Thus, the DBMS can use these functions for parallel execution. For UDAF there is currently no possibility to register additional local and global aggregation functions. This is the reason, why a UDAF like the MOST_FREQUENT function cannot be executed with the usual two step parallel aggregation scheme.

Another problem is that current ORDBMS do not allow the developer to define a special partitioning function for a UDAF. However, unfortunately not all UDAF can be processed in parallel on all kinds of partitions as we will show later. The latter is also valid with respect to scalar functions that have an input context. In some cases, the result will be semantically incorrect if the data partitioning does not take the semantics of the function into consideration.

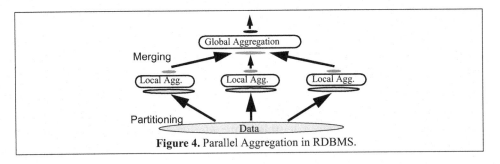

Figure 4. Parallel Aggregation in RDBMS.

We can summarize the discussion as follows: UDSF with an input context and all practical UDAF cannot be processed in parallel without special support by the DBMS. This situation will result in a performance bottleneck in parallel ORDBMS query processing. In shared-nothing and shared-disk parallel architectures the input data is often distributed over various nodes and must be shipped to a single node to process a UDF with input context correctly, i.e., sequentially, and afterwards the data possibly has to be redistributed for further parallel processing. This results in additional communication costs and hence even worse performance.

3.3 Parallel Processing of UDF

In this section, we describe several orthogonal approaches to enhance the parallel processing of UDF with an input context. In subsection 3.3.1 we introduce local and global aggregation functions for UDAF as a generalization of the relational processing scheme. In subsection 3.3.2 we introduce partitioning classes and define the class of partitionable functions that can be processed with data parallelism. In subsection 3.3.3 we propose sorting as a preprocessing step to enhance the parallel execution for non-partitionable UDAF. Subsection 3.3.4 contains corresponding syntactic extensions to the DDL statements for the registration of UDF.

3.3.1   Two Step Parallel Aggregation of UDAF

In this subsection we will show how aggregates can be processed in two steps using local and global aggregate functions.

To simplify the presentation below, we will omit constant input parameters to UDF. Given a set S, we will use shorthand notations like f(S) for the resulting aggregate value of an aggregate function f applied to S. We will also use the notation f(S) to denote the result of repeatedly invoking a scalar function f for all elements of S. We want to emphasize that in this case f(S) denotes a multi-set of values (a new column).

Next, we define the class of aggregate functions that can be processed in parallel using local and global aggregation functions. An *aggregate* function f is *partitionable* iff two aggregate functions f_l and f_g exist, such that for any multi-set S and some partition S_i of S, $1 \leq i \leq k$, the following equation holds:

$$f(S) = f_g(\cup_{1 \leq i \leq k} \{f_l(S_i)\}) \qquad \text{(EQ 2)}$$

The notation f_l indicates that the function is applied *locally* (for each partition), whereas f_g is applied *globally*. In addition the result size of the local function f_l must be either bound by a constant or it must be a small fraction of the input size. This requirement is important, since otherwise one could use the identity as local function and the sequential aggregation function as the global function. Clearly, this is not desirable, since it would not improve processing. In general, the smaller the size of the local results, the better the speedup that can be expected, as there is less data to be exchanged and less input for the global aggregation. Obviously, if an aggregate function is partitionable, the local aggregate function can be executed for all partitions S_i in parallel, while the global aggregation must be processed sequentially.

If an aggregate function is used in combination with grouping, the optimizer can also decide to process several groups in parallel. In this case grouping can be done with the algorithms described in [99]. The algorithms discussed there can be applied orthogonally to our approach. Of course, if enough parallelism is possible by processing different groups in parallel, the optimizer might decide that no further parallel processing of the aggregate function is needed.

One disadvantage of this two step approach to parallel aggregation is that we are not always able to apply one aggregate function to both sequential and parallel processing. Therefore the developer might have to implement and register six additional functions (Init, Iter, and Final functions for local aggregation and the same for global aggregation) to enable parallel as well as sequential processing of a UDAF. However, if one does not need maximum efficiency for sequential evaluation, one can simply use the local and global functions for sequential execution, too. This, however, will incur at least the overhead for the invocation of an additional function. On the other hand, the additional work for the developer will pay off with all applications that profit from the increased potential for parallelism. Besides that, there seems to be no solution that results in less work for the developer.

3.3.2   Partitioning Classes and Partitionable Functions

One prerequisite for data parallelism is that one has to find a suitable partitioning of the data. This means that the partitioning must allow a semantically correct parallel processing of the function. In order to ease the specification of all partitionings that are correct for the parallel processing of a UDF, we describe a taxonomy of the functions that can be used for data partitioning.

All partitioning functions take a multi-set as input and return a partition of the input multi-set, i.e., a set of multi-sets such that any element of the input multi-set is contained exactly in one resulting multi-set. Actually in some cases we will allow functions returning subsets that are not disjoint, i.e., functions that replicate some of the elements of the input set. We define the following increasingly more special classes of partitioning functions:

- ANY: the class of all partitioning functions. Round-robin and random partitioning functions are examples that belong to no other class. All partitioning functions that are not based on attribute values belong only to this class.
- EQUAL (column name): the class of partitioning functions that map all rows of the input multi-set with equal values in the selected column into the same multi-set of the result. Examples of EQUAL functions are partitioning functions that use hashing.

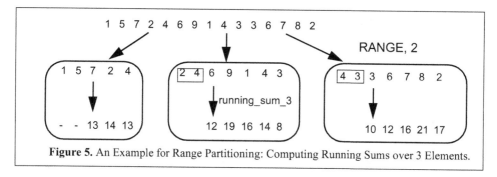

Figure 5. An Example for Range Partitioning: Computing Running Sums over 3 Elements.

- RANGE (column name [, N]): the class of partitioning functions that map rows, whose values of the specified column belong to a certain range, into the same multi-set of the result. Obviously there must exist a total order on the data type of the column. The range of all values of the data type is split into some sub-ranges that define which elements are mapped into the same multi-set of the resulting partition. Based on the total order of the data type the optional parameter N allows to specify that the largest N elements of the input set which are smaller than the values of a certain range have to be replicated into the resulting multi-set of this range. Replicated elements must be processed in a special way and are needed only to establish a "window" on a sorted list as a kind of global context for the function. The number of elements that belong to a certain range should be much greater than the value N. This class of partitioning functions is especially useful for *scalar* functions that require a sorted input, for example scalar functions that compute moving averages or running sums (see subsection 3.4.4). An example for range partitioning with replication of two elements (N=2) is shown in Figure 5. It is used to compute the running sum of the three most recently seen elements of the input set. In the example there are three partitions and replicated elements are shown inside rectangles in the second and third partition.

Please note that the following inclusion property holds: RANGE ⊂ EQUAL ⊂ ANY. This taxonomy is useful to classify UDF according to their processing requirements as we will see below. The database system can automatically provide at least a partitioning function of class ANY for all user-defined data types (e.g. round-robin). We define that a *class C partition* of a multi-set is a partition that is generated using a partitioning function of class C (C denotes either ANY, EQUAL or RANGE).

Based on these definitions we can now define the classes of partitionable aggregate and scalar functions. These classes describe the set of UDF that can be processed in parallel with the usual execution schemes for data parallelism (cf. Figure 3 and Figure 4) and a particular class of partitioning functions.

A *scalar* function f is *partitionable for class C* iff a function f_l exists, such that for any multi-set S and any class C partition S_i of S, $1 \leq i \leq k$, the following equation holds:

$$f(S) = \cup_{1 \leq i \leq k} f_l(S_i)$$

(EQ 3)

A scalar function f that is partitionable for class C using the associated function f_1 can be evaluated in parallel using the following scheme, given a multi-set S and a partitioning function p of class C:

1. Partition S in k subsets S_i, $1 \leq i \leq k$, using p.
   Distribute the partitions to some nodes in the system.
2. Compute $f_1(S_i)$ for $1 \leq i \leq k$ for all S_i in parallel.

Figure 6. Parallel Processing Scheme for Partitionable Scalar Functions.

An *aggregate* function f is *partitionable for class C* iff two functions f_1 and f_g exist, such that for any multi-set S and any class C partition S_i of S, $1 \leq i \leq k$, the following equation holds:

$$f(S) = f_g(\cup_{1 \leq i \leq k} \{f_1(S_i)\})$$ (EQ 4)

The schemes in Figure 6 and Figure 7 show how partitionable functions can be processed in parallel. All k partitions can be processed in parallel. The actual degree of parallelism (i.e., mainly the parameter k) has to be chosen by the optimizer as usual. Please note that for the scheme in Figure 6, there is not always a need to combine the local results. Hence, the optional combination step (computing $f(S) = \cup_{1 \leq i \leq k} f_1(S_i)$) is left out. In order to enable the DBMS to process a UDF in parallel the developer must specify the allowed partitioning class when the function is registered (cf. subsection 3.3.4).

We have introduced some extensibility to the traditional parallel execution schemes by parameterizing the partitioning step by means of the partitioning function. In addition, we have defined classes of partitions to allow the optimizer more flexibility w.r.t. to the choice of the partitioning function. The query optimizer can try to avoid data repartitioning, when multiple UDF are processed, if the developer specifies only the class of the partitioning functions. For example, if two UDSF f and g must be processed, f is registered with ANY and g with EQUAL, then both functions can be parallelized with a partitioning function of class EQUAL. In general, the optimizer has to find a partitioning function in the intersection of the partitioning classes of all functions that occur in a given query. Computing the intersection is easy due to the inclusion property between the classes (However, one must also consider the columns that are used for partitioning). This can reduce processing costs dramatically, especially for shared-disk and shared-nothing architectures. If the developer specifies a single partitioning function for each UDF, in almost all cases a repartitioning step will be needed to process several UDF in parallel. Vice versa, if a single partitioning function satisfies all of the partitioning classes of a given set of UDF, then repartitioning can be avoided.

Because UDF can have arbitrary semantics, we believe that it is not possible to define a fixed set of partitioning functions that allows to apply data parallelism to *all* UDF. If a given UDF is partitionable using some partitioning function p, but none of

An aggregate function f that is partitionable for class C using the two associated functions f_l and f_g can be evaluated in parallel using the following scheme, given an input multi-set S and a partitioning function p of class C:

1. Partition S in k subsets S_i, $1 \leq i \leq k$, using p.
   Distribute the partitions to some nodes in the system.
2. Compute $I_i := f_l(S_i)$ for $1 \leq i \leq k$ for all S_i in parallel.
   Send all intermediate results I_i to a single node for processing of step 3.
3. Compute $f(S) := f_g(\cup_{1 \leq i \leq k} \{I_i\})$;
   f_g can be applied to the intermediate results I_i in arbitrary order.

Figure 7. Parallel Processing Scheme for Partitionable Aggregate Functions.

the partitioning classes defined above, the developer should be enabled to specify that this function p must be used. We call this function p *user-defined partitioning function*. However, using a special partitioning function should be avoided in general, since all data has to be repartitioned before such a UDF can be processed.

We want to remark here that implementing RANGE partitioning is a bit complicated, since a user-defined sort order and partial replication have to be supported. One difficulty is for example to find equally populated ranges for a given user-defined sort order. We believe that range partitioning with partial replication can be best supported by an appropriate extension of the built-in sort operator of the ORDBMS. This operator has to support user-defined sort orders anyway. The definition of ranges and partial replication can be supported, if information about the data is collected during the sorting process.

In addition to that extension, the operator that invokes UDSF has to be extended. The UDSF that needs the range partitioning is evaluated immediately after the partitioning. Replicated data elements (that have to be marked) are processed by the UDSF in a special mode that has to be indicated by turning on a special switch. In this mode only the global context of the UDSF is initialized and no results are produced. For example, when the moving average over five values is computed, the first four values of a partition will be replicated ones and are stored in the global context of the function. Then, the fifth invocation produces the first result. Though this extension is conceptually simple, it may be difficult to add it to an existing engine.

3.3.3   Parallel Sorting as a Preprocessing Step for UDAF

Some user-defined aggregate functions can be easily implemented, if their input is sorted according to a specified order. In this case the sort operation can be executed in parallel. Of course, this is especially interesting for UDAF that are not partitionable.

> An aggregate function f that requires a sorted input can be evaluated using the following scheme given input multi-set S:
> 1. Sort the input S. This can be done in parallel.
> 2. Compute f(S) without parallelism (use early termination, if possible).
>
> **Figure 8.** Parallel Processing Scheme for Aggregate Functions with Sorted Input.

Sorting as a preprocessing step for UDAF can be introduced by using an additional parameter in the CREATE FUNCTION statement (see subsection 3.3.4 for details of the syntax we propose). Of course the developer must have the possibility to specify a user-defined order by providing a specific sort function for the argument data types of the UDF which are often user-defined data types. In most cases such functions will be needed anyway, to support sorted query results, to build indexes (like generalized B-Trees ([102], [104]) or GiSTs [46]) or for sort merge joins to efficiently evaluate predicates on user-defined data types, to quote some examples.

One interesting point to observe is that many aggregate functions, which operate on a sorted input, do not need to read the complete input set to compute the aggregate. Thus, it might be well worth to provide the aggregate function with the option to terminate the evaluation as early as possible and return the result. We call this feature *early termination*. The parallel processing scheme for aggregate functions with sorted input is shown in Figure 8.

The optional sort requirements can be integrated into rule-based query optimization (see e.g. [30], [36], [67], [73]) simply by specifying the sort order as a required physical property for the operator executing the UDF. Then a sort enforcer rule ([30], [38]) can guarantee this order requirement by putting a sort operation into the execution plan, if necessary. Informix Illustra [53] already supports optional sorting of inputs for UDF that have two arguments and return a boolean value. The developer can specify a user-defined order for the left and right input of such a function. Obviously this allows to implement a user-defined join predicate using a sort-merge join instead of a Cartesian product followed by a selection. Thus, our proposal can be seen as an extension of this approach w.r.t. to a broader class of supported UDF and their parallel execution.

3.3.4   Extended Syntax for Function Registration

In this subsection, we present the syntax extensions for the statements that allow the registration of UDF with support for the features introduced in the previous subsections.

```
CREATE FUNCTION <function-name> (<argument type list>)
RETURNS <data type name>
EXTERNAL NAME <external function name>
[ORDER BY {<argument name> [USING <sort function name>] [ASC | DESC] }
[EARLY TERMINATION]]
[ALLOW PARALLEL WITH PARTITIONING CLASS (
     ANY
   | EQUAL (<argument name list>)
   | RANGE {<argument name> [, <number>]
           [USING <sort function name>] [ASC | DESC]}
   | <partitioning function name> )]
LANGUAGE <language name>
. . .
```

Figure 9. Extensions to the DDL Statement for UDSF Registration.

Figure 9 shows the extensions for the CREATE FUNCTION statement. We have marked our extensions by boldface. The ORDER BY clause can be used to specify a sort order that is required for the input table, on which the function is executed. The input table can be sorted on multiple columns applying user-defined sort functions to define the sort order. Furthermore, the developer must specify if early termination is used. To enable parallel evaluation, the partitioning class has to be specified. In addition to ANY, EQUAL and RANGE partitioning, the developer can register a special (user-defined) partitioning function for a UDF.

Figure 10 shows the extensions for the CREATE AGGREGATE statement. It now includes the local and global function options that are needed to register the aggregate functions that have to be used for the parallel evaluation of the new aggregate function. Of course the various Init, Iter, and Final functions that are registered must be consistent w.r.t. their argument types. For example the sequential and the global Final functions must have the same return types (but often will have different argument types)

As we mentioned already in chapter 2 additional information about these functions should be supplied by the developer. In addition to the usual cost parameters, information about the size of the results of the local aggregation function (perhaps depending on the cardinality of the input set, if the function returns a collection type or LOB) would be desirable.

```
CREATE AGGREGATE <function-name> (
<Init, Iter, and Final function definition>
[local <Init, Iter, and Final function definition> ]
[global <Init, Iter, and Final function definition> ]
)
```

Figure 10. Extensions to the DDL Statement for UDAF Registration.

3.4 Example Applications

In this subsection, we present some example applications to illustrate the benefits of the introduced techniques.

3.4.1   The UDAF Most_Frequent

First, we will demonstrate how parallel execution can be enabled for the aggregate function Most_Frequent. How can we use the two step processing scheme to process the function Most_Frequent in parallel? A straightforward approach could be to compute the most frequent value for each partition in parallel using the local aggregate function. This implies that the local aggregate function returns the most frequent value together with the number of its occurrences (i.e., the return type of the local function contains two values). Then the overall most frequent value is computed by the global function. Obviously this scheme is only correct if EQUAL is specified as the partitioning class for the local aggregation function. If ANY would be used as a partitioning class, the local aggregate function would have to return *all distinct* values together with the number of their occurrences for each partition. Thus, the local aggregation step would not be useful.

One difficulty of this approach is to implement the local aggregation function, since it must temporarily store *all* distinct values together with a counter. It is difficult to implement this efficiently in a user-defined function, since the function must be able to store an arbitrarily large data set. By contrast, the local aggregation can be done much easier if the developer uses sorting as a preprocessing step. The function must then only store two values and two counters: one for the most frequent value seen so far and one for the last value seen. This approach is much more practical. Based on the syntax from subsection 3.3.4 we show the registration of the Iter function for the local aggregation ('$i' denotes the argument at position i in the parameter list of the function).

```
CREATE FUNCTION
ITER_MF_LOCAL(POINTER, INTEGER)
RETURNS POINTER
EXTERNAL NAME 'libfuncs!mf_iter_local'
ORDER BY $2 ASC
ALLOW PARALLEL WITH PARTITIONING CLASS EQUAL $2
LANGUAGE C ...;
```

With EQUAL as partitioning class in case of a parallel execution the data is first partitioned and then only the partitions are sorted as specified in the ORDER BY clause.

```
SELECT MIN(Age)
FROM Persons AS P
WHERE (SELECT Ceiling((COUNT(*) + 1) / 2) FROM Persons)
<=
(SELECT COUNT(*) FROM Persons AS R WHERE R.Age <= P.Age)
```

Figure 11. Computing the Median in Relational SQL.

3.4.2   The UDSF Running_Average

As an example of a UDSF with input context, we discuss the function
Running_Average. This function computes for each input value the average of the
N values seen last. This means that the input context of the function is a 'window' of
size N. Thus, the function Running_Average is partitionable of class RANGE with
parameter N. Obviously the function Running_Average computes many aggregates with a single scan over the input table. This is a typical example of a UDSF
with an input context. Other functions of that kind are for example available in Red
Brick Systems' Intelligent SQL [94].

3.4.3   The UDAF Median

As an example of a function that seems to be non-partitionable consider the Median
function that computes the $\lceil (N+1)/2 \rceil$ largest element of a set with N elements (that
element could be informally called the 'halfway' element). A query that finds the
median of a set is not very intuitively expressible in SQL-92. For example, the simple query to select the median of the ages of certain persons could be expressed as
shown in Figure 11. Of course one would prefer a query using a UDAF Median as
shown in Figure 12.

```
SELECT Median(P.Age, COUNT(*))
FROM Persons AS P
```

Figure 12. Computing the Median in Object-Relational SQL.

The object-relational query is not only easy to write, but will also run more efficiently, because the function Median can be implemented with lower complexity
than the complex query in Figure 11 as we will show in the following. The function
Median is called with two parameters (cf. Figure 12): the first parameter is an element of the already sorted input set, the second parameter is constant and gives the
cardinality of the input set[1]. When the function is called the first time, it computes

---

1.   Some systems do not support nesting of aggregate functions. In this case one could e.g. use a sub-
      query in the FROM clause to compute the cardinality.

the median position and stores this position in the global context. In addition the function maintains a counter for the number of invocations. During each call the function checks whether the median position is reached. In this case, the function stores the input value in the global context. Because the input is sorted, this value is actually the median of the input set. Finally, the function returns the median. Figure 13 demonstrates this algorithm for a set of integers. Obviously this function is easy to implement, because essentially it has to scan its input until the right position has been reached. This implementation has an asymptotic complexity of $O(N*\log(N))$ due to sorting, while the computation with the SQL query from Figure 11 has one of $O(N^2)$. In case of the function Median using the early termination option would save roughly half of the calls to the function.

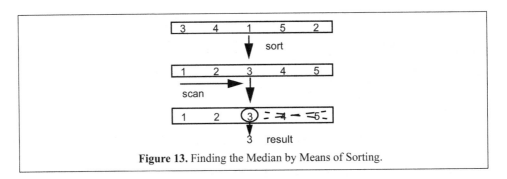

Figure 13. Finding the Median by Means of Sorting.

3.4.4   Further Applications

In this section, we apply the concept to some additional UDF shown in Table 1. The table contains also the three examples that we have discussed in detail in the previous subsections. The first five aggregate functions of the SQL-92 standard have well known semantics and need not to be explained. However, we want to emphasize that in an ORDBMS a function like the SUM function can be defined for any data type available. For example some RDBMS support time durations as a data type, but no sum function that allows to sum up durations easily. Using our framework such a sum function can be defined and executed in parallel.

The other functions that are shown in Table 1 may need some explanations. GCD denotes the greatest common divisor (gcd). The gcd is the intersection of the prime factors of a set of integers. Hence, we can compute the function GCD in parallel, by computing this intersection first locally and then globally for the local results. The Variance function computes the square of the statistical variance of a set S of sample values v_j given the arithmetic mean m of these values as a constant parameter. The partial sums s_i given here are computed as $\sum_j (v_j - m)^2$; $v_j \in S_i$ (with $S_i \subset S$). The Nth_largest function selects the Nth largest element of a sorted set. N is a

Table 1. Characteristics of Some User-Defined Functions

UDF	Scalar Function	Sorted Input	Partitioning Class	Sequential Implementation	Local Implementation	Global Implementation
MAX	N	N	ANY	max	max	max
MIN	N	N	ANY	min	min	min
SUM	N	N	ANY	sum	sum	sum
COUNT	N	N	ANY	count	count c_i	sum{c_i}
AVG	N	N	ANY	average	sum s_i; count c_i	sum{s_i} / sum{c_i}
GCD	N	N	ANY	gcd	gcd	gcd
Variance	N	N	ANY	variance	sum s_i; count c_i	sum{s_i} / sum{c_i}
Nth_largest	N	N	ANY	Nth largest	N largest (set)	Nth largest
Shape_sum	N	N	ANY	shape sum	shape sum	shape sum
Closest	N	N	ANY	closest	closest	closest
N_Tile(N)	N	N	ANY	N_tile	count higher values h_i; count c_i	$\lfloor$(sum{h_i}/ sum{c_i}) *N$\rfloor$ + 1
Most_Frequent	N	Y	EQUAL	most frequent	most frequent	most frequent
Median	N	Y	-	scan position	-	-
Rank	N	Y	EQUAL	rank	local rank	global rank
Cumulative	Y	Y[a]	-	cumulative	-	_[b]
Running_Sum(N)	Y	Y[a]	RANGE (N)	running sum	running sum	_[b]
Running_Avg(N)	Y	Y[a]	RANGE (N)	running avg.	running avg.	_[b]

a. A sorted input (possibly with a user-defined sort order) is needed due to the semantics of this function.
b. Global functions are not applicable to UDSF.

parameter of the function. Please note that the local functions have to return the *subset* consisting of the N largest elements, while the global function just returns the Nth largest *element* and is the same as the sequential implementation. The `Shape_sum` function is an aggregate function that returns the geometric union of shapes like polygons or rectangles (e.g. bounding boxes). The `Closest` function computes one of the nearest neighbors in a set of geometric objects in a common coordinate system for a given point in this coordinate system. The function N_Tile computes the number of the interval (also called tile) to which a given value belongs. The values of the input column are first grouped into N intervals that have roughly the same cardinality. Then the interval to which the given input value belongs is computed and the rank of this interval is returned. For example, if we compute the N_Tile for N = 10 and if the value belongs to the highest 10 percent of all values or is higher, then the result is 1. If the given value is lower than all values in the column, the result is 11. We can parallelize this function with a partitioning of class ANY and compute the number of higher values h_i as well as the number of all values c_i locally within each partition. Based on these local counts and the value N, we can compute to which interval the given value belongs using the formula that is given for the global implementation in Table 1.

The functions `Most_Frequent` and `Median` have been discussed already. The function `Rank` computes the rank of a given value within the N values of a column. If the value is higher than all values in the column, its rank is 1; if it is lower than all values, its rank is N+1. If we use a partitioning of class EQUAL and sort the input set, we can first compute the local ranks of the given value for each partition. We can then compute the global rank as the sum of the L local ranks minus (L-1). Hence, we can compute the rank completely in parallel.

The last three functions in Table 1 are scalar functions with a scratchpad that need a sorted input due to their semantics. The function `Cumulative` computes the running sum over all values seen so far, whereas the function `Running_Sum(N)` computes the running sum of the N most recently seen values. The function `Running_Avg(N)` was already discussed. All three functions operate on a sorted list. This is necessary, since their result depends on the order in which the input values are seen. There seems to be no possibility to compute the function `Cumulative` in parallel, because the input context of this function consists of all values seen so far. On the other hand, the functions `Running_Sum(N)` and `Running_Avg(N)` are partitionable with a partitioning function of class RANGE (N) including replication of N values. We want to emphasize that these functions must not return a value (not even NULL) for replicated input values to guarantee the same number of result tuples as in sequential processing.

In summary, these examples show that the parallel evaluation of many UDF can be supported using the introduced techniques, because they are actually partitionable. All example functions are partitionable or use a sorted input. Therefore they can either be executed completely in parallel or they can use parallel sorting.

3.5 Plausibility Considerations Regarding Performance

We will now discuss the possible performance benefits for processing partitionable UDAF in our framework. Basically we provide a first assessment of the obtainable performance of parallel UDF processing that should make the efficiency of our framework more plausible. Note that these considerations are straightforward for partitionable UDSF. We use the obtainable speedup of the parallel execution of a UDAF to estimate the efficiency of our approach. It has to be emphasized that we compare the sequential and parallel execution of the aggregation function only, i.e., we do not try to estimate the speedup for the evaluation of complete queries.

For our analysis we use a simple analytic cost model that takes only CPU costs into consideration. This seems to be roughly appropriate to us as the aggregated size of main memories tends to increase on a parallel system compared to a uniprocessor system. Thus, the necessary I/O will almost always be less in the parallel case. CPU costs for communication can be quite significant for parallel evaluation, but will vary to a great extent depending on the architecture used. For example in shared-everything systems the costs for exchanging intermediate results between processors are negligible, if shared memory is used properly. We do not expect that communication bandwidth will be a problem given the rapid progress in networking technology (consider e.g. a switched gigabit network or an ATM-based network). Therefore we will also ignore bandwidth problems for the moment. The costs of computing the UDAF f sequentially may be different from the costs when using f_g and f_l for sequential evaluation, but in order to keep our model simple we assume that these costs are nearly equal (i.e., cost (f_l) + cost (f_g) ≈ cost (f)). Thus, our cost model has the following three components:

1. F:
   CPU cost for evaluating the UDAF. $F = $ cost (f_l) + cost (f_g) ≈ cost (f)

2. P(d):
   CPU cost for data partitioning depending on the degree of parallelism d, i.e., the number of different nodes that process a partition.

3. I(d):
   CPU cost for exchange of intermediate results depending on the degree of parallelism d.

The cost for the sequential execution of the UDAF is simply F. The cost for the parallel execution is F + P(d) + I(d). When using parallel execution the input streams will often be already partitioned on different nodes, and without the possibility to evaluate the UDAF in parallel all the data has to be shipped to a single node. Therefore the cost P(d) will be low in most cases when compared to a sequential evaluation of the UDAF. I(d) depends on the size of the sub-aggregates and hence on the implementation of the specific UDAF at hand. If the size of the intermediate results is low compared to the size of the input set, the relative costs I(d) are quite low. Thus, the obtainable speedup SP (depending on the degree of parallelism d) can be approximated roughly as follows:

$$SP(d) = \frac{\text{sequential execution time}}{\text{parallel execution time}} = F / [(F + P(d) + I(d))/d] \approx d*F/F = d$$

This approximation is especially useful, if the UDAF is expensive, i.e., if F >> P(d) + I(d).

In summary, we have seen that a near-linear speedup can be expected in many cases. Thus, our framework for parallel processing can be advantageous for the overall query processing time. Whether or not parallelism for UDAF should be used for a given query is a cost-based decision the optimizer has to make. The same is true for partitionable scalar functions, too.

3.6 Related Work

User-Defined Functions (UDF) have attracted increasing interest of researchers as well as industry in recent years (see e.g. [3], [17], [45], [47], [68], [70], [83], [89], [98], [102], [104]). Despite this, most of the work discusses only the non-parallel execution of UDF. We see our contribution as a generalization and extension of the existing work on the execution of user-defined functions using data parallelism. Recently, IBM added the optional clause ALLOW PARALLEL or DISALLOW PARALLEL to the create function statement for UDSF in DB2 UDB [50]. We view this as a first step of support for parallel execution of UDSF that is consistent with our more comprehensive framework. To the best of our knowledge there is no work on parallel processing of scalar user-defined functions with an input context.

In [29] and [99] parallel processing of aggregate functions in RDBMS has been studied. The proposed concepts are applicable to built-in aggregation functions and consider also aggregation in combination with GROUP-BY operations and duplicate elimination. The proposed algorithms in [99] may be combined with our framework, if user-defined aggregate functions are used with GROUP-BY. It has been observed in [29] that different local and global functions are needed for parallel aggregation operations in RDBMS. In [89] the concept to process user-defined aggregate functions in parallel using two steps is proposed as a general technique, but neither are details nor more sophisticated processing techniques (like sorting as a preprocessing step, early termination or partitioning classes) presented. Recently, Informix added a two-step scheme for parallel aggregation to their Universal Data Option [95]. Their design is similar to ours, however they need only 4 functions (only one init and final function, whereas we use two: one for the local and one for the global function). In [76], RDBMS are extended by ordered domains, but neither is an object-relational approach taken nor are functions considered.

It is interesting to compare our classification of aggregate functions in partitionable and non-partitionable aggregate functions with other classifications. In [33], a classification of aggregate functions into three categories is developed primarily with the goal to be able to determine, if super-aggregates in data cubes can be computed based on sub-aggregates for a given aggregate function. It is pointed out that this classification is also useful for the parallel computation of user-defined aggregate functions. In the classification that is proposed in [33] an aggregate function f with a given input multi-set S and an *arbitrary* partition S_i of S is:

- *distributive* iff there is a function g such that

$$f(S) = g(\cup_{1 \le i \le k} f(S_i)). \tag{EQ 5}$$

- *algebraic* iff there is an M-tuple valued function g and a function h such that

$$f(S) = h(\cup_{1 \le i \le k} g(S_i)). \tag{EQ 6}$$

It is pointed out that the main characteristic of algebraic functions is that a result of fixed size (an M-tuple) can summarize sub-aggregates.

- *holistic* iff there is no constant bound on the size of the storage needed to represent a sub-aggregate.

Clearly, distributive and algebraic functions are both partitionable aggregate functions for the partitioning class ANY. Note that our definition of partitionable aggregate functions is less restrictive with regard to the size of the sub-aggregates. Aggregate functions that are easy to implement using a sorted input are typically holistic. Aggregate functions that are partitionable with a less general partitioning class than ANY, e.g. the function MOST_FREQUENT, are holistic in this scheme, but can be evaluated in parallel by our framework. Other holistic functions like e.g. the function Median can be efficiently evaluated in our approach, by using parallel sorting as a preprocessing step and early termination. Note that the application scenario in [33] is different to ours with regard to partitioning and parallel evaluation, because the sub-aggregates in data cubes must be computed for fixed partitions that are determined by semantically defined sub-cubes and not by the application of some partitioning function. The classification of Gray et al. was designed with the goal to compute data cubes efficiently. However, the rationale behind our work was to find a classification of functions that is useful for parallel evaluation.

In [111] the class of decomposable aggregate functions is introduced to characterize the aggregate functions that allow early and late aggregation as a query optimization technique. This class of aggregate functions is identical to partitionable aggregate functions of partitioning class ANY except that no size restriction for sub-aggregates is required in [111]. Thus, for these partitionable functions also certain rewrite optimizations are possible that provide orthogonal measures to improve the performance. In [16] the class of group queries is identified for relational queries. This class is directly related to data partitioning. Our framework provides support for the concept of group queries in object-relational processing as well.

3.7 Summary

In this chapter we have proposed a framework that allows parallel processing of a broad class of user-defined functions with input context in ORDBMS. This is an important step in removing a performance bottleneck in parallel object-relational query processing.

Since it was clear that a straightforward application of data parallelism is not possible, we had to devise more sophisticated parallelization techniques. The three key techniques that we have proposed here are the following: First, we have generalized the parallel execution scheme for aggregation in relational systems by means of local and global aggregations to allow its application to user-defined aggregations. Second, we have introduced some extensibility to the parallel execution schemes for scalar and aggregate functions by means of user-defined partitioning functions. We have defined classes of partitioning functions to make the specification of all allowed partitioning functions easier and to enable the optimizer to avoid data repartitioning as much as possible. Third, we have introduced parallel sorting as a preprocessing step for user-defined aggregate functions. This enables an easier implementation of UDF and the use of parallelism in the preprocessing phase. Furthermore, we have defined new interfaces that allow developers to use these techniques by providing the needed information to the DBMS.

As a summary Table 2 shows the different kinds of contexts that can occur for UDF and the implications for parallel execution with respect to data parallelism. As can be seen from Table 2, our techniques support data parallelism with respect to many, but not all UDF with input context. Additional techniques might emerge in the future. Please note that a general solution for UDF with external context is beyond the scope of this work.

Table 2. UDF with Different Contexts and their Parallel Execution

	scalar functions	aggregate functions
no context	partitionable for class ANY	(not reasonable)
input context	partitionable for some class	partitionable for some class with local and global aggregation
		parallel sorting (& early termination)
	not partitionable	
external context	not treated here	

An important remaining question with respect to the parallel execution of UDF is the following: How can we execute a UDF that operates on a single LOB in parallel? The next chapter is dedicated to the solution of this problem.

CHAPTER 4

Intra-function Parallelism

4.1 Introduction

In this chapter we focus on intra-function parallelism for expensive functions that operate on large objects (LOBs). Intra-function parallelism means that the invocation of a scalar function which operates on a single LOB is computed in parallel. Intra-function parallelism is orthogonal to data parallelism and hence this kind of parallelism can still be exploited, if data parallelism is not applicable. In this chapter we present an approach to enable intra-function parallelism in PORDBMS. Since LOBs can be used to implement collection data types like arrays and sets that are proposed for future SQL standards, our technique to enable intra-function parallelism might be useful for parallel processing of collection types as well.

As pointed out in [85] intra-function and inter-function parallelism are important, because many object-relational extensions support expensive functions on large data objects. The reason is that LOBs are used to implement a rich variety of new data types, for example in applications which deal with multimedia, financial or spatio-temporal data. Some of these data types like digital photos, satellite images and video data have a really huge size. For example, currently a single high resolution digital photo has a size of 18 MB. Note that in current commercial systems (see for example [50], [54], [86]) large data types ranging to tera byte sizes are supported. Moreover, one can expect that computationally expensive scalar functions are used to extract knowledge from such LOBs or to transform these LOBs. Hence, processing a single large object like a satellite image or a video film already consumes significant resources. Unfortunately neither data parallelism nor pipeline parallelism can be employed for the processing of a *single* large object. In the rest of this chapter, we discuss how intra-function parallelism can be used to overcome this limit of current PORDBMS and to speed up query processing further.

This chapter is organized as follows. Section 4.2 presents our approach to intra-function parallelism and section 4.3 contains a performance study that shows the viability and the benefits of our approach. Section 4.4 covers the related work and section 4.5 summarizes the chapter.

M. Jaedicke: Parallel Object-Relational Query Processing, LNCS 2169, pp. 33-44, 2001.
© Springer-Verlag Berlin Heidelberg 2001

4.2 Compose/Decompose Operators for Intra-function Parallelism

In this section we describe our approach to intra-function parallelism for expensive user-defined scalar functions on LOBs. The rationale of our design is the following: first, a necessary requirement is that the application of intra-function parallelism remains completely transparent for users of UDSF in SQL statements. Second, the design should provide developers of UDSF with a model of intra-function parallelism that combines ease of use with the highest possible degree of flexibility.

4.2.1 Compose/Decompose Operators

The basic idea of our approach is shown in Figure 14. The left side of Figure 14 shows the state of the art. A UDSF F is processed sequentially on a LOB (the white box) and returns another LOB (the hatched box). We propose to enable intra-function parallelism by means of two new database operators: a decompose and a compose operator. This is depicted on the right side of Figure 14. First the decompose operator is applied to the LOB which results in a set of pieces of this LOB (the small white boxes in Figure 14). Then the UDSF F is invoked for each of these pieces. Some or all of these invocations can be done in parallel (indicated by the two operator instances for the evaluation of the UDSF F in Figure 14). The result is a set of modified LOB pieces (the small hatched boxes in Figure 14). Finally the compose operator assembles the LOB from the pieces. Hence, in general a UDSF can be computed in parallel by adding a pair of decompose/compose operators that encloses the evaluation of the function.

One might expect that the use of decompose and compose operators incurs a high overhead. But in fact this is not the case if LOB locators (cf. subsection 2.2.4) are used properly. If the size of the LOB is significantly larger than the size of the locator, then the overhead for the decompose and compose operations is relatively low as we show in the following. Because in most applications the size of the LOB will usually be some orders of magnitude larger than the size of the LOB locator (which is for example less than 312 Bytes in DB2 UDB [50]), the overhead is usually acceptable.

Typically a developer will code the UDSF in such a way that not the LOB itself is passed as a parameter, but the LOB locator. In this case the LOB locator can be used to access some or all LOB data using positioned access. Similarly the UDSF will return a locator that refers to the result LOB and not the result LOB itself. The decompose operator can work in the same way: instead of reading the entire LOB and returning a set of LOB pieces, it is sufficient to work with LOB locators. This means that we pass a LOB locator to the decompose operator. The decompose operator simply makes N copies of the LOB locator and attaches to each copy the number

N and a unique number K between 1 and N as access information. The numbers N and K describe the piece of the LOB on which the UDSF should work. Hence, the result of the decompose operator is a collection of rows. This corresponds exactly to the functionality of a correlated table function (cf. subsection 2.2.3 and [50]). The compose operator uses the values of N and K to determine how to construct the result of the LOB. Please note that the number of pieces (N) is a parameter for the decompose operator that is provided by the optimizer (cf. subsection 4.2.3 below).

In this approach, a copy of the LOB locator and the corresponding access information are passed as parameters to the UDSF. The UDSF can infer from the value of K on which of the N pieces it should operate. Therefore, the developer has to explicitly consider that the UDSF might operate only on a part of a LOB and that access information is passed to the UDSF as two additional, internal parameters (these parameters are not visible in SQL statements and, if no decomposition is done, i.e., if no intra-function parallelism is used, then these parameters have NULL values). Then, the UDSF normally accesses only the part of the LOB that is described by the access information. This is usually easy to integrate into the code of the UDSF. The reason is that the UDSF will typically use the locator to fetch only a small portion of the LOB at the same time into main memory. This kind of processing is necessary to limit main memory requirements. Please note that providing a copy of the locator for the *complete* LOB as a parameter to the UDSF has the following benefit: if the partial result of the UDSF cannot be computed by looking only at the specific piece of the LOB then the UDSF can read further LOB data as needed. Therefore our approach supports intra-function parallelism for a broad range of UDSF. The compose operator can exploit LOB locators in a similar way. The use of copies of complete LOB locators is important to support a maximum of flexibility for developers of UDSF as discussed in the next section.

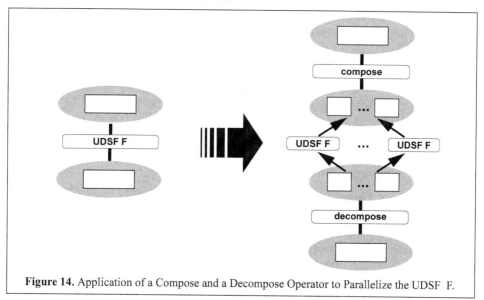

Figure 14. Application of a Compose and a Decompose Operator to Parallelize the UDSF F.

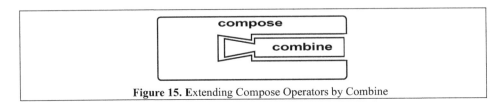

Figure 15. Extending Compose Operators by Combine

Finally, we want to point out that the decompose/compose operators work with the usual tuple streams that allow to pass data from one operator to the next. The LOB locators and the values N and K are fields of the tuples and can be handled as usual. The LOBs themselves are accessed only from within the body of the UDSF and are therefore not themselves included into tuple streams. Hence, the handling of intermediate results is not affected by decompose and compose operators.

4.2.2   Extensibility of Compose Operators by Combine Functions

In this subsection, we explain how compose operators can be made extensible. The compose operator should be extensible itself with respect to the way in which LOBs are assembled. This is necessary to allow developers to deal with the semantic differences of various data types and functions.

Such a kind of extensibility can be achieved by providing a user-defined *combine function* to the compose operator. This is shown in Figure 15. The combine function tells the compose operator how the LOB can be assembled from the pieces. The system has to provide default combine functions that work on the different kinds of LOBs (BLOBs, CLOBs, DBCLOBs) without taking data semantics into account. Sometimes a single combine function might suffice for all UDSF that operate on a LOB data type, but in general there can be a specific combine function for each UDSF that operates on a LOB data type. Please note that in the latter case the combine function is tailored to the specific UDSF and can be used to complete the computation of the UDSF during the combination. This can be necessary, if the UDSF cannot be computed completely by invoking it only for each piece of the LOB. In this case the UDSF is computed in two steps: first, the UDSF is invoked for each piece and second, the combine function is executed during the compose operation. This approach is similar to the divide-and-conquer strategy that can be used to compute (user-defined) aggregates in parallel (cf. chapter 3).

In the example of Figure 14 we have assumed that the UDSF returns a LOB. This assumption is not necessary. In fact, with user-defined combine functions the decompose/compose-approach can be used for *all* UDSF that operate on LOBs because the combine function can compute the correct return value.

We provide now a very simple example of a UDSF that needs a combine function to support intra-function parallelism. Consider the UDSF:

```
CREATE FUNCTION count_char(CLOB text, CHAR(1) c)
RETURNS INTEGER ...
```

that counts how often the character c occurs in a given text. We can implement intra-function parallelism in the following three steps:

1. Decompose the CLOB into N pieces. This step is done by the decompose operator.

2. For each piece in parallel: count how often the character c occurs. This step is implemented by the UDSF count_char.

3. Add the counts for all pieces and return the sum. This is the functionality of the combine function that is invoked by the compose operator.

In order to implement this approach, developers must be enabled to create combine functions that can be applied to the instances of a certain LOB data type. Because combine functions are user-defined functions, too, no special support for this is needed (that is, the combine function can be registered as a UDSF). However, it is necessary to register a new UDSF with parameters that allow the developer to specify *which* combine function has to be used to enable intra-function parallelism for this UDSF. For example an optional clause like "DECOMPOSABLE [USING <combine function name>]" could be added to the CREATE FUNCTION statement for the registration of UDSF. If no specific combine function is specified, the system can use the default combine functions for BLOBs, CLOBs, or DBCLOBs.

Please note that in our approach a similar extensibility for the decompose operator is *not* needed. The reason is that the decompose operator simply makes copies of the locator for the *complete* LOB. Therefore the UDSF can decide itself, which portion of the LOB should be accessed for the processing of a given piece. This kind of virtual decomposition allows a maximum flexibility.

4.2.3   Application of Intra-function Parallelism

In our view intra-function parallelism is best applied by a rule-based optimizer (for example [30], [36]). Such an optimizer has to be extended my means of a rule that inserts appropriate pairs of compose/decompose operators. Obviously, the compose/decompose operator pair should be only inserted by the optimizer, if it estimates that the application of intra-function parallelism reduces the response time.

Intra-function parallelism can reduce the response time, if data parallelism is not sufficient to speed up processing. This is the case, if the number of LOBs that have to be processed with a UDSF is less than the number of available CPUs. For example, if we have a multi-processor but only a single LOB. The question is how to determine the number of pieces (i.e., the parameter N) into which a LOB should be decomposed. If the cost of the function is significantly higher than the overhead for intra-function parallelism (that is, if either the function evaluation is expensive or the

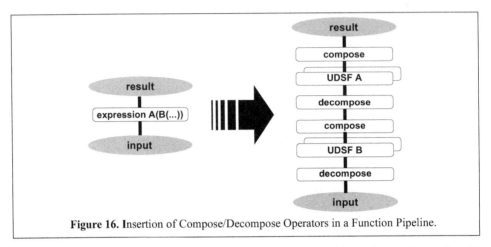

Figure 16. Insertion of Compose/Decompose Operators in a Function Pipeline.

LOBs are huge), then the number of pieces can be set roughly to the number of available CPUs (the exact value might be system-dependent). In general, as our measurements in the following section 4.3 show, a number of pieces that is much higher than the number of CPUs does not result in a significant overhead. In general a thorough cost-based decision should be needed only, if the UDSF is cheap to compute or if an expensive user-defined combine function has to be used. In both of these cases, intra-function parallelism might not be useful at all.

Of course, if a UDSF operates only on a small part of the LOB data, then intra-function parallelism should not be used. In this case the developer should not register the UDSF as decomposable.

4.2.4   Intra-function Parallelism for Function Pipelines

In this subsection, we will consider the case that we have a pipeline of functions that can be processed with intra-function parallelism. This applies for example, if two UDSF A and B are nested in an expression like A(B(...)). As it is shown in Figure 16 one can now insert a pair of decompose/compose operators around each function. This allows intra-function parallelism for both functions.

In some cases it is possible to optimize this scenario further by an elimination of the compose and decompose operators between the UDSF A and B. However, this is not possible in general and requires additional support. The reason is that the combine and decompose operator are needed to generate copies of the LOB locator for the *complete* result LOB of UDSF A which is the expected input for the evaluation of UDSF B.

4.3 Experimental Performance Study

We have evaluated our approach by implementing the functionality of decompose and compose operators on top of IBM's DB2 Universal Data Base, Version 5, running on SUN Solaris V2.5 for a simple UDSF that operates on a CLOB (cf. [40]). The goal of these measurements was to show the feasibility of this approach. That is, we wanted to show that performance gains can be achieved in some scenarios. A real implementation within a core parallel data base system would have been too expensive in relationship to the additional insight into this topic that could have been gained. One reason for this is that a sophisticated, high performance implementation of LOBs with locators in a PORDBMS is needed. Such implementations are already available in commercial products [63], but for example they are not available in our PORDBMS prototype MIDAS [9]. Without a suitable implementation of LOBs with locators, the overhead of the decompose/compose approach would be unrealistically high. The disadvantage of an implementation on top of a commercial system is that the overhead for communication between client and server is significant and limits the speedup. Hence, this implementation cannot show the full benefit of compose/decompose operators.

All measurements have been made on a SUN SPARC 20 symmetric multi-processor machine (SMP) with four SPARC processors with 100 MHz each, 128 MB main memory and a disk array with four 4.2 GB hard disks. We have used a SMP for our measurements, because we see that commodity SMPs become available and that the scalability of SMPs improves. Therefore, we believe that intra-function parallelism will be used primarily on SMPs. In a hybrid shared-nothing architecture (in which the nodes are SMPs) data parallelism can be used for processing on different nodes and intra-function parallelism can be used for parallel processing on a single SMP node. This is possible due to the orthogonality of the parallelization concepts.

4.3.1 Experimental Scenario and Implementation

For our performance study we have considered a UDSF on a CLOB because this seemed to be favorable to development. As UDSF we have implemented a function `invert` that inverts the characters within the CLOB (that is A is changed into Z, B into Y, etc.). To be able to increase the cost of this simple function we have added an empty for-loop that is executed once for each character and increments the loop variable 100 times. We have then generated random character strings and stored them as CLOBs in a table `clobtable` with two columns: a column `id` that contains a primary key and a column `text` that contains the CLOB.

We have implemented two programs that perform essentially the following task: one or more CLOBs are selected from the `clobtable` and then the function `invert` is applied to these CLOBs. The result is then inserted into a persistent table in the database.

The first program without decompose/compose operators performs essentially the following insert statement (see appendix A.1 for the complete program):

```
INSERT INTO result (id, text)
SELECT id, invert(text,1,1)
FROM clobtable
WHERE id < param;
```

The value of param is constant and used only to select a specified number of CLOBs from the clobtable. For example, if param has the value 4 then the number of selected tuples - each containing a CLOB - is 4. In the following, we call this program sequential_in-vert.

The function invert was registered with the DBMS as follows:

```
CREATE FUNCTION invert (CLOB(150M) AS LOCATOR text, INTEGER piece,
                        INTEGER num_pieces)
RETURNS CLOB(150M) AS LOCATOR ...;
```

This function accepts three parameters: first the locator of the CLOB that should be inverted. The second parameter corresponds to the number of the LOB piece (cf. the variable K in subsection 4.2.1). The third parameter contains the number of pieces into which a LOB is decomposed (cf. the variable N in subsection 4.2.1). Since we cannot use intra-function parallelism in the program sequential_invert, the values for the parameters are always $N = K = 1$. Please note that the parameters N and K would not be visible for users in SQL statements. However, in our case of an on-top implementation this was unavoidable.

The second program implements the operation in a way that comes close in effect to the decompose/compose operator approach. Our first approach to implement the decompose operation was to use a UDTF that generates the necessary number of copies of the CLOB locator. Unfortunately, we found no way to execute the resulting statement with the UDTF in parallel. Therefore we have simply used a join with another persistent table (named join-table) that contains exactly N rows for each LOB. Each of these N rows consists of two integer values: the first value (id1) corresponds to the id of the CLOB, the second (id2) contains a unique number in the range $1, 2, \ldots, N$ and is used to give each piece a unique identifier (that is, it serves as value for the parameter K). The latter value is used as a parameter for the function invert. The following statement shows the decompose operation and the application of the function invert (for $N = 4$):

```
SELECT a.id + 0 AS id1, b.id2 + 0 AS id2, invert(a.text,b.id2,4) AS text
FROM clobtable AS a, jointable AS b
WHERE a.id = b.id1
ORDER BY id1, id2;
```

We have to explain here, why we have used an ORDER BY clause and the two additions in the SELECT clause. The compose operation could have been easily written as a user-defined aggregate operation. But DB2 UDB V5 does not support this feature. Therefore, we used a cursor to fetch locators of the pieces and assembled the result using the system-provided concatenation operator ('||'). For this approach, it was most efficient to sort the pieces by their number. This ensures that all pieces of one LOB arrive in order. Hence, only one LOB is assembled at a time. However, since id is the primary key of the table `clobtable` the optimizer decided to use an index scan for an ordered access to the base table. While this avoided the sort operation, it also forced sequential execution. Therefore, we introduced the additions to prevent the optimizer from using the index access. Appendix A.2 shows the complete program `parallel_invert`.

4.3.2   Performance Results

We have conducted a series of performance measurements to show the effect of decompose/compose operations.

Experiment 1: Speedup with Decompose/Compose Operators

In the first experiment, we have studied the effect of the number of LOB pieces and the degree of parallelism for the processing of a single CLOB of size $10*10^6$ Byte (i.e., ten million characters). This LOB size is moderate and we have used a version of the function invert with higher cost to increase the overall costs: for each character in the CLOB, the function inverts the character as mentioned above and increments a counter 100 times.

Figure 17a shows the response time (in seconds), if we use the value 4 as a default degree of parallelism for the programs. In this case the DBMS tries to execute all statements with this degree of parallelism, that is, it employs 4 processes to execute the function invert. This is only possible for the select query that is executed in the program *parallel_invert*. The parallelism is actually only useful, if more than a single piece is generated for processing.

As one can see in Figure 17b, the best speedup that can be achieved is about 2.7. This is less than the optimum speedup value 4. However, we can expect this, as not all 4 processors can be used exclusively to process the test program because of the operating system and DBMS overhead. An even more important limit for the speedup is however that we use a program on-top of the DBMS for the implementation. All work on the client side and the client/server communication represent thus a part of the program that cannot be executed in parallel. This limits the overall speedup significantly according to Amdahl's law [2] and is an important reason for the less than optimal speedup. Therefore when the decompose/compose operators are integrated into the execution engine a better speedup can be achieved.

Furthermore, as Figure 17 shows, the response time depends in some rather unforeseeable way on the number of pieces into which the CLOB is decomposed. We have

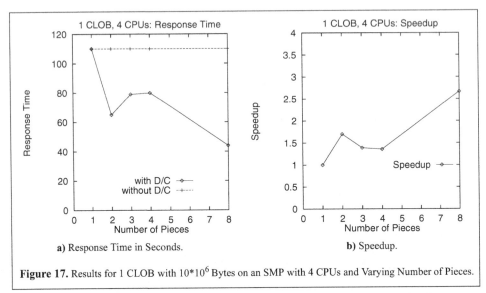

a) Response Time in Seconds.   **b)** Speedup.

Figure 17. Results for 1 CLOB with $10*10^6$ Bytes on an SMP with 4 CPUs and Varying Number of Pieces.

not been able to determine the reason for the changes in the system behavior. However, while the response time is influenced by the number of pieces, the *overhead* from copying the LOB locators for an increasing number of pieces has not a dramatic effect on the overall performance. This is clearly demonstrated by the results in Table 3. Here we show the response times for 1 CLOB with 4, 8, 16, and 40 pieces, respectively. In all of these cases, the DBMS used all 4 CPUs for parallel query execution. Ideally the response time should be roughly the same in all cases. Differences should result only from the overhead for creating a higher number of copies of LOB locators. However, as the measurements show, the response time is not determined by this overhead. In our view, it seems that the handling of LOBs within the data base engine does not yet fully support the requirements for intra-function parallelism. This again demonstrates that an integration of decompose/compose operators into the database engine would be even more beneficial. In general, the results show that decompose/compose operators can support intra-function parallelism appropriately.

Table 3. Response Times in Seconds for a Varying Number of Pieces

number of pieces	4	8	16	40
response time	80	44	61	48

Experiment 2:   Trade-Off between Intra-function Parallelism and Data Parallelism

In another experiment, we have considered the execution of the UDSF for several CLOBs at a time to study the trade-off between intra-function parallelism and data parallelism. All CLOBs had the same size ($1*10^6$ Bytes) and they were all processed with the same function. Figure 18 shows response times and speedups for the processing of a varying number of CLOBs in the programs. Figure 18a shows that intra-function parallelism with decompose/compose operations can provide an additional speedup, if data parallelism alone cannot fully utilize system resources. This is the case for the processing of up to 3 CLOBs. Figure 18b shows that the actual speedup is lower than the optimal speedup. This is due to the same reasons as in the first experiment. For 4 CLOBs, when data parallelism alone can achieve a degree of parallelism of 4, additional intra-function parallelism results in a small overhead. However, if the size of the CLOBs varies considerably, intra-function parallelism might be desirable even for 4 or more CLOBs. The reason is that the decomposition reduces the skew for data parallelism that results from LOBs with different sizes.

In general these results show that intra-function parallelism can be beneficial, if the number of LOBs is lower than the number of available CPUs. In this case intra-function parallelism can supplement data parallelism as demonstrated by the second experiment. We want to emphasize again that an implementation of the decompose/compose approach within the database engine would show a much better performance than indicated by our on-top implementation.

4.4 Related Work

In [85] intra- and inter-function parallelism were proposed for expensive function evaluations on LOBs, but no implementation concepts were described. As an example of a UDSF for which intra-function parallelism is useful, a function that scales large images up or down is discussed. It is pointed out that this function can be processed in parallel because the result pixels are all independent of each other. Our

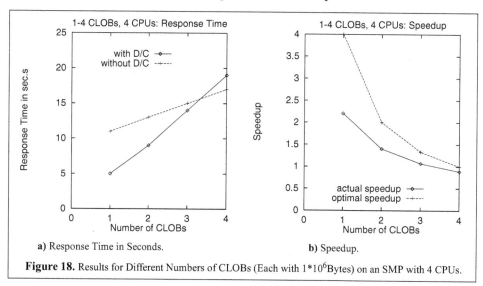

a) Response Time in Seconds.   **b)** Speedup.

Figure 18. Results for Different Numbers of CLOBs (Each with $1*10^6$Bytes) on an SMP with 4 CPUs.

decompose/compose operator method can support even functions for which this is not the case. If the UDSF needs to access overlapping parts of a LOB when different pieces are processed, this is possible, since all instances of the UDSF get the locator for the complete LOB as input. Moreover, if the different parts of the result are not completely independent then the combine function can be used to achieve an appropriate composition of the pieces.

In [28] parallel processing of operations on complex data structures (for example with sets of references) is discussed. This is done in the framework of the PRIMA DBMS which has a proprietary data model. UDSF are not considered.

4.5 Summary

In this chapter, we have proposed decompose/compose operators as an approach to support intra-function parallelism for user-defined scalar functions that operate on large objects. This approach was designed to be orthogonal to data parallelism. Initial measurements have shown that our concept looks promising and can lead to a good speedup. For example, the results showed significantly improved response times, if the number of LOBs is lower than the number of available CPUs and if the UDSF is expensive.

Our system design and evaluation as presented in this chapter clearly shows two important results: First, our approach based on decompose/compose operators fits into current database engines. However, to achieve maximum benefit, it should be integrated into the DBMS engine. Second, our implementation shows that this parallelization concept is applicable right now as a solution on top of commercial PORDBMS.

With respect to future work, we believe that the applicability of decompose/compose operators for the case of collection data types that are internally implemented by means of LOBs deserves some further study because this would enable data parallelism for operations on collection data types.

In chapters 3 and 4 we have introduced new techniques for the parallel execution of UDF. While these measures can speed up response times considerably, we have not changed the concept of UDF and their implementation in a fundamental way. In the next chapters we present new approaches to extensible query processing that try to use the semantics of UDF to speed up set-oriented operations during query processing. One important goal is to avoid Cartesian products, if UDPs are available as join predicates. In this case user-defined join algorithms can improve the response times by orders of magnitude as we will demonstrate. Because set-oriented operations are the core of query execution, this issue is in our view very important.

CHAPTER 5

The Multi-operator Method

5.1 Introduction

Though the move to PORDBMS emphasizes the demand for high performance in object-relational query-processing, some techniques for efficient query processing that have been very successful in relational query processing are still missing. One obvious example is the support for join algorithms. There has been a lot of research on joins in RDBMS (see e.g. [29], [72] for a survey), but this topic has not been covered in depth for ORDBMS. The state of the art is essentially that user-defined join predicates in ORDBMS are evaluated by performing a nested-loops join that evaluates the user-defined predicate on the Cartesian product. A similar approach in RDBMS would make all queries with equi-joins awfully slow. In ORDBMS the performance is deteriorated even further, since user-defined predicates are often extremely expensive to evaluate. Thus, an evaluation of these predicates on the full Cartesian product (even if not materialized) results in unacceptable performance.

In the context of special application areas, there has been some research on efficient join algorithms for data types like spatial or temporal data (see e.g. [11], [87], [88], [112]). Unfortunately, some of these techniques cannot be integrated well into current ORDBMS. The reason is that the current implementation model for user-defined functions is too simple to allow for sophisticated implementations.

Our main contribution in this chapter is to propose the multi-operator method as an implementation technique to solve these fundamental problems. The multi-operator method allows to integrate complex implementations of user-defined functions and predicates in ORDBMS with the best possible support for parallel evaluation. The basic idea of the multi-operator method is to use multiple operators instead of a single one. This results into a simple, yet powerful technique. We believe that it offers the potential for immense performance gains for many object-relational applications. Performance measurements that we present later will demonstrate this.

Our approach fits well into the overall architectural framework of current parallel ORDBMS. In fact to enable the use of this method, ORDBMS have to support only

M. Jaedicke: Parallel Object-Relational Query Processing, LNCS 2169, pp. 45-66, 2001.
© Springer-Verlag Berlin Heidelberg 2001

an interface that allows the execution of a query execution plan that is specified by the developer. Thus, we are convinced that this method is easy to use for developers and can be supported in ORDBMS without major difficulties. In fact, as we will discuss later, there are other reasons for database vendors to support this kind of interface.

The remainder of this chapter is organized as follows. We give an introduction to the problem in section 5.2. The multi-operator method is presented in section 5.3 and we discuss a spatial join algorithm as an example application. Section 5.4 considers the interface that is necessary to make the multi-operator method available in ORDBMS. In section 5.5 we report on performance measurements for our spatial join example which indicate significant performance gains. We cover the related work in section 5.6 and conclude the chapter with a summary in section 5.7.

5.2 Performance Problems with Complex UDF in Current ORDBMS

We claim that there is currently not enough support for the efficient implementation of complex UDF in ORDBMS. We will demonstrate this in the following using a spatial join as an example of a complex UDP. Our example is the following spatial query, which selects all pairs of polygons from a single table that overlap with each other:

```
select    *
from      Polygon_Table a, Polygon_Table b
where     overlaps(a.p_geometry, b.p_geometry)
```

How is this query evaluated in a current commercial ORDBMS? Let us assume that no spatial indexes can be used to evaluate the join predicate overlaps. Because this is not a traditional join (like an equi-join), no system will use a hash or a merge join. Hence, all ORDBMS will use a nested-loops join for evaluation, i.e., the UDP overlaps has to be evaluated on the full Cartesian product. Please note that in this scenario data parallelism can be applied to the nested-loops join by partitioning the outer input stream and replicating the inner input stream (at least, if the system supports data parallelism for UDF). In general the developer must be able to disallow such a parallel evaluation, since the function that implements the UDP might have a global state or side effects, as we have discussed in chapter 3. In fact, most sophisticated algorithms have such a global state or side effects, since it is often necessary to hold temporary data.

Despite of the parallel evaluation the performance of this straightforward approach is poor. It is known that a much better performance can be achieved, if a filter-and-refine approach ([11], [87], [88], [112]) is taken. This approach uses two phases: the filter phase finds pairs of candidates for the result using a relatively inexpensive test. This test is only a rough filter in the sense that some false candidates can pass the test. All candidate pairs are therefore tested with the original join predicate (the overlaps predicate) in the refinement phase. It has been observed in the literature that this approach results in a much better performance, as the filtering reduces the input for the refinement phase significantly and the latter is the most expensive one. Typically the test in the filter phase is not evaluated using the exact geometries. Rather a simple approximation like the bounding box is used for the test. This reduces the CPU costs for the test and also reduces the storage requirements considerably. We will provide more details in the following subsection.

5.2.1   The PBSM Algorithm as a Sophisticated UDP Implementation

We will now use the Partition Based Spatial-Merge Join algorithm (PBSM) proposed in [88] for a detailed example. We want to emphasize again that we are not aware of a practical way for developers of DBMS class libraries [13] to implement such a sophisticated algorithm in any ORDBMS. It is the goal of the multi-operator method to make this possible with full support for parallel evaluation.

The PBSM algorithm is based on a two-phase filter-and-refine-scheme and is processed sequentially, though the authors of [88] believe that it can be parallelized efficiently. We will first give an outline of the algorithm (cf. Figure 19). The input of the PBSM are two sets of spatial object geometries (like polygons). It is assumed that each spatial object can be identified via an OID. We will assume that the spatial join predicate is the `overlaps` function. We will number the steps of the algorithm using numbers in brackets like [1.1]. The first number denotes the phase, the second one the step within this phase.

The first phase is the filtering phase. It begins with creating key-pointer elements (step [1.1]), i.e., (MBR, OID) pairs, where MBR denotes the minimum bounding rectangle. These key-pointer elements are then written to temporary tables on disk (step [1.2]). Next a decision is made (step [1.3]): if the temporary relations fit into main memory, the algorithm proceeds with step [1.4], otherwise with step [1.5]. In step [1.4] the candidate pairs are computed using the MBRs and a filter algorithm. The filter algorithm is based on plane-sweeping techniques from computational geometry and is viewed as a kind of spatial-merge join in [88]. This set of candidate pairs forms the input for the refinement phase. In step [1.5] the data for the filter step is first partitioned. This begins with an estimation of the spatial universe (the MBR of all spatial input objects) using data from the system catalog. Step [1.6] decomposes this universe into P subparts. Given this partitioning of the space, the corresponding spatial data partitioning function is applied to the temporary tables that contain the key-pointer elements (step [1.7]). Finally, partitions with the same index

---

1. Filtering Phase

1.1   Create key-pointer elements, i.e., (MBR, OID) pairs;

1.2   Write key-pointer elements to temporary tables on disk;

1.3   IF (temporary tables fit into main memory)

1.4   { Compute candidate pairs using the MBRs and a filter algorithm }
       ELSE

1.5   { Estimate the spatial universe;

1.6   Decompose this universe into P subparts;

1.7   Apply the resulting spatial data partitioning function to the
           temporary tables that contain the key-pointer elements;

1.8   Apply the filter algorithm to partitions with the same index
       };

2. Refinement Phase

2.1   Remove duplicates in the set of candidate pairs;

2.2   Sort the OID pairs on the OID of the first input;

2.3   WHILE (not all candidate pairs have been processed)

2.4   { Fetch a subset of the base data of the first input
           that fits into main memory;

2.5   Swizzle the corresponding OIDs to main memory;

2.6   Sort the corresponding OIDs of the other input;

2.7   Read the tuples corresponding to these OIDs
           sequentially from disk;

2.8   IF (exact join predicate holds) append tuple to output
       }

Figure 19. Outline of the PBSM Algorithm.

---

are processed with the filter algorithm (step [1.8]). This produces the set of candidate OID pairs for the refinement step.

The second phase, refinement, proceeds as follows. First, duplicates in the set of candidate pairs are removed (step [2.1]). Such duplicates can occur, since the key-pointer elements are partially replicated during the partitioning to deal with spatial objects overlapping several partitions as shown in Figure 20. In step [2.2] the OID pairs are sorted on the OID of the first input (this will avoid random I/O). While there are still candidate pairs that have to be processed (step [2.3]), the algorithm performs steps [2.4]-[2.8] as follows: a subset of the base data of the first input is fetched that fits into main memory (step [2.4]) and the corresponding OIDs are swizzled to main memory (step [2.5]). Next the corresponding OIDs of the other input are sorted (step [2.6]). The tuples corresponding to these OIDs are then read sequentially from disk (step [2.7]). Finally, a tuple is appended to the output, if the exact join predicate (i.e., overlaps) holds for the candidate pair (step [2.8]).

Please note that the PBSM algorithm must manage intermediate results, retrieve objects based on their OID and partition data using a special partitioning scheme.

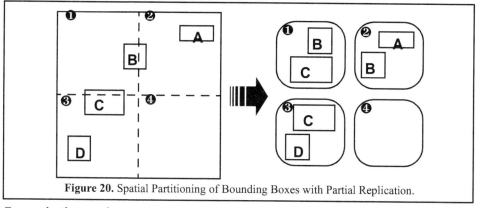

Figure 20. Spatial Partitioning of Bounding Boxes with Partial Replication.

Currently there exists no technique that allows developers to integrate an algorithm with such features into an ORDBMS in a way that enables a completely parallel execution. Note that the complexity of the PBSM algorithm is by no means an exception. As pointed out in [89] for the geo-spatial application domain, complex UDF often consist of multiple steps.

5.3 The Multi-operator Method as a New Technique to Implement Complex UDF

Next we will describe our approach to overcome the performance problems discussed in the previous section. We introduce the multi-operator method in subsection 5.3.1 and discuss its principal benefits. Subsection 5.3.2 illustrates the method by studying a multi-operator implementation of the PBSM algorithm as an example.

5.3.1   The Multi-operator Method and Its Benefits

The basic idea of the multi-operator method is quite simple. Current ORDBMS allow the implementation of a UDF only by means of a function that is (repeatedly) invoked within the execution of a *single* operator (e.g. a restriction, projection or a nested-loops join) of a query execution plan. By contrast, we will allow an implementation by means of several functions that are invoked by *multiple* operators (i.e., by an operator graph, where the operators may invoke several other UDF).

This method can be viewed as an extension and generalization of the well-known implementation scheme used in relational engines for sort-merge joins. Here, instead of a single operator typically three operators are used to implement this join algorithm: one sort operator for each of the inputs and an operator for the merge join. There are at least three good reasons for this design. The first reason is that a sort operation is needed for other purposes (like producing a sorted output), too. Thus, this operator can simply be *reused*. The second reason is that sometimes an input stream may already arrive sorted from previous operations - in this case no sort is needed and the superfluous sort operation can be eliminated. In general, *optimizations* of the query execution plan are enabled. The third reason is that using three operators instead of one allows to use more *parallelism*. For example, the two inputs can be sorted in parallel by means of the highly optimized system-provided parallel sort operation. All of these arguments - reuse, optimizability, and parallelism - are in our view applicable to multi-operator implementations of UDF in general. This is not so much surprising, given that the operator concept is one of the basic abstractions and building blocks used in query execution. Therefore replacing a single complex operator by a set of simple ones offers the possibility for improved query execution plans due to the finer granularity that is introduced.

As we will show below in detail, a multi-operator implementation supports all kinds of parallel execution, i.e., intra-operator parallelism, pipelining, independent parallelism, and intra-function parallelism. If a traditional implementation by means of a single function is used, it is often impossible to execute the operator containing this function with data parallelism due to the complexity of the UDF implementation (e.g. side effects, storage of temporary data). A multi-operator implementation allows the developer to code the UDF in a set of operators, where each operator can possibly be executed in parallel and where the DBMS knows the dataflow between the operators. We believe that the multi-operator method provides the developer with the right method to offer the DBMS an implementation that can be executed in parallel, since operators are a natural granule for parallel execution in relational database systems ([22], [29]).

The multi-operator method can achieve especially high performance gains when it is applied to UDPs that can serve as join predicates as described in section 5.2. In this case, a multi-operator implementation will allow to replace the standard execution plan consisting of a Cartesian product and a restriction with the UDP by a multi-operator implementation of that UDP that is a user-defined join algorithm that exploits multiple operators and several UDF. It is easy to see that this will enhance the performance of many object-relational queries, when one considers the importance of joins in relational systems: without the various highly optimized join algorithms that avoid Cartesian products for the most commonly used join predicates like e.g. equality predicates, relational systems would have been hardly successful in the marketplace.

Figure 21 shows a schematic view of a multi-operator implementation for a UDP. Without special support a UDP is evaluated by means of a nested-loops join on the complete Cartesian product as shown on the left side of Figure 21. A complex UDF often executes a number of steps, here N. The multi-operator implementation allows to perform a number of processing steps (K steps in Figure 21) before the two input relations are actually joined. Thus, a part of the UDP can be pushed down. Please

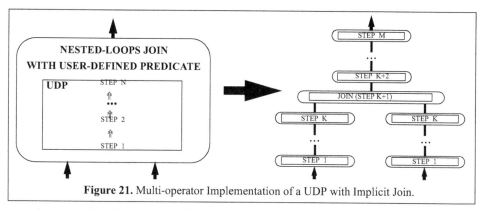

Figure 21. Multi-operator Implementation of a UDP with Implicit Join.

note that now the Cartesian product can be avoided. Instead, a specialized join algorithm (Step K + 1 in Figure 21) can be used. After the join some postprocessing is done. In general, the preprocessing steps will have often the goal to map user-defined data types to approximations (sometimes also called features) that are represented by built-in data types. These approximations can then be processed with the traditional built-in operators to perform a filter step. The postprocessing steps then do the refinement based on the results of the filter step.

Note that the number of steps in the single-operator (N) and the multi-operator implementation (M) may differ as already mentioned before. In general the design of both implementations may vary significantly. If the developer does a careful design, parallelism can be exploited to a full extent in the multi-operator implementation.

5.3.2   A Multi-operator Implementation of the PBSM Algorithm

To provide a detailed example application of the multi-operator method, we will now discuss, how the PBSM algorithm from subsection 5.2.1 can be redesigned and mapped to a multi-operator implementation (no details concerning the integration of PBSM into Paradise [89] are given in [88], but it seems to be implemented by a new database operator). Of course, one goal of such a redesign should be to allow as much parallelism as possible for the multi-operator implementation. Figure 22 shows a multi-operator implementation of a simplified version of the PBSM algorithm. In the first step, the key-pointer elements are generated for both inputs. These key-pointer elements are then partitioned. It is necessary to have a common spatial partitioning for both input streams to be able to compute the join by joining only corresponding partitions. The next operator joins the partitions and generates the candidate pairs. This corresponds to step [1.8] of the PBSM algorithm. The second phase, refinement, starts with the duplicate elimination. Then the next two operators fetch the exact geometries from disk using the OIDs. Finally, the spatial join predicate is evaluated on the exact geometries for each candidate pair.

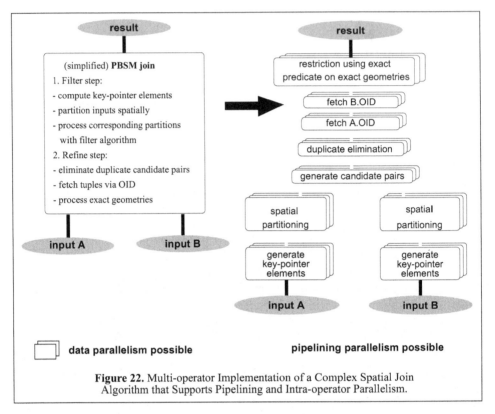

Figure 22. Multi-operator Implementation of a Complex Spatial Join Algorithm that Supports Pipelining and Intra-operator Parallelism.

Several remarks w.r.t. the multi-operator implementation are in order. Our redesign did really simplify the PBSM algorithm: there is no decision on the processing strategy based on the amount of temporary data (cf. step [1.3] above). In a parallel processing scenario this is desirable, since it avoids a blocking of the evaluation, until the decision is made. Furthermore, the refinement step was simplified substantially, as there are no efforts to avoid random I/O. Though this will lead to higher resource requirements for disk I/O, we believe it is much harder to avoid random I/O, if parallel evaluation is used. There are also two major advantages of the overall design. First, pipelining parallelism can be applied between all operators. Second, data parallelism can be used for all operators. Especially, the join and the very expensive predicate in the refinement phase can be evaluated in parallel (see Figure 22).

When one compares this implementation with the original PBSM as described above, it is obvious that all control structures (like conditional statements and loops, cf. steps [1.3] and [2.3] in subsection 5.2.1) have been eliminated. As a direct benefit, query parallelization as known from traditional relational DBMS is enabled and in addition the processing model of relational execution engines is matched perfectly.

This example clearly shows that a multi-operator implementation increases the potential for parallelism in query execution plans. Thus, it allows to implement efficient join algorithms for UDPs that can be evaluated in parallel by existing object-relational execution engines.

5.4 Supporting the Multi-operator Method

The multi-operator method fits well into current system architectures. We want to point out here that its implementation in a commercial ORDBMS requires no changes in the core data base system. It is only necessary to add a new interface to the current APIs (like embedded SQL, ODBC and JDBC) that allows the execution of a query execution plan that is specified by the developer.

In the following we will first argue why we believe that such an interface is useful for current DBMS anyway. In subsection 5.4.2 we describe then the interface that we have used.

5.4.1   Executing Query Execution Plans

We believe that there are several reasons why an interface that allows the specification and execution of query execution plans is needed. We want to emphasize that such an interface will only be used in addition to SQL, not as a replacement. In our opinion this interface will typically be used by sophisticated developers of third party software vendors that produce packaged applications like enterprise resource planning software, geographic information systems, CAD software, etc.

The first reason is that very often developers have the problem that they know an execution plan that is better than the plan that is generated by the optimizer. There are many reasons for this situation like, for example, erroneous selectivity estimation. Currently there is only the possibility to view the plan that the optimizer has generated. If this plan is not the desired one, one must then try to manually transform the corresponding SQL statement until one reaches a more satisfying result. This process needs some exercise and can be both time-consuming and disappointing. There is a further shortcoming of this approach in practice. When vendors upgrade their DBMS they often improve their optimizer somehow. While such improvements may be beneficial for most queries they can degrade the performance of some others - maybe just the important ones. Therefore developers face the problem that the optimizer might change the plan of the 'tuned' SQL query in the next release. Moreover the choice of the concrete execution plan might also depend on database statistics and the settings of the various tuning knobs of the DBMS both of which may vary from customer to customer. This makes it pretty hard to guarantee a good performance for a specific query and to provide customer support. Obviously all these problems can be avoided if the execution plans are specified by the developer. On the other hand all these particular situations could be taken care of by a comprehensive and sophisticated optimizer. However, such an optimization technology is not (yet) available. Hence, it can be seen as a conceivable strategy by some vendors to add support for this feature.

The second reason for supporting query specification at the plan level is that the full power of the query execution system cannot be exploited by SQL. For example, it is well-known that in SQL sorting can only be used in the outermost query block. This is too restrictive in specific situations (cf. subsection 3.3.3). When developers can specify query execution plans directly they can go beyond these limits.

We believe that these issues themselves justify the extension of the current APIs. The multi-operator method adds just another reason, why such an interface is highly desirable. However, there is also a drawback of this approach, if we add no further enhancements: without any query optimization, i.e., when the query execution plans are executed exactly as specified by the developer, the plan is not automatically adapted to changes of the database like a drastically increased table size or changing value distributions. An improvement of this situation is to allow the DBMS the optimization of *some, but not all properties* of a manually specified execution plan. For example, one can allow the optimizer to remove superfluous sort operators, or to optimize the join order, or to optimize the implementation methods of the plan (e.g. switch from merge join to hash join), or to choose a different access path (using a table scan instead of an index scan). In a rule-based optimizer like Cascades [30] this can be supported by grouping the rule set into subsets. Then only some subsets of the whole rule set (for example only the rules that eliminate superfluous sort operators) are activated when a manually crafted plan is optimized. In this case, the developer must be enabled to specify which properties of the plan can be optimized. Such specifications can be viewed as optimizer hints (cf. [3], [53], [86]).

One could object that it is difficult for a developer to come up with a plan for a complex query which involves many tables, many predicates and subqueries. However, the developer can always use a query execution plan that is generated by the optimizer as a starting point. This plan can then be modified by the developer. For example, this allows to start with a join order that the optimizer considers as good for a given database.

There are different ways how query execution plans can be specified. One possibility is to store plans in tables (query explain tools of some vendors do this already [50]) and then allow developers to update these plans and execute the modified ones. In the following, we describe a different interface that is based on a textual description of operator trees.

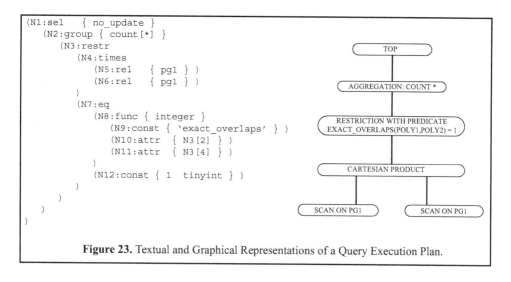

```
(N1:sel    { no_update }
   (N2:group { count[*] }
      (N3:restr
         (N4:times
            (N5:rel    { pg1 } )
            (N6:rel    { pg1 } )
         )
         (N7:eq
            (N8:func { integer }
               (N9:const { 'exact_overlaps' } )
               (N10:attr  { N3[2] } )
               (N11:attr  { N3[4] } )
            )
            (N12:const { 1  tinyint } )
         )
      )
   )
)
```

Figure 23. Textual and Graphical Representations of a Query Execution Plan.

5.4.2   Example for a Textual Specification of Query Execution Plans

In MIDAS [9], our prototype of a parallel object-relational DBMS, execution plans can be specified in a text notation for internal test and debugging purposes. Parentheses form the boundary of the textual description of each node of the operator graph. Each node has a unique label and contains the name of its operation and additional parameters. The sons of a node are nested within the description of the node itself. One can refer to the attributes of the input tuple of another node by using the label of this node.

Figure 23 shows the textual description of a query execution plan together with the corresponding operator graph as an example. The `sel` node represents the top operator of SELECT queries. The `group` operator does grouping and aggregation and the `times` operator builds a Cartesian product. The `restr` operator performs a restriction, the `rel` operator does a relation scan. The `eq` node specifies an equality predicate, the `const` node generates a constant value and the `attr` node fetches an attribute value. Finally, the `func` node allows to evaluate a (user-defined) function. Of course syntactic and semantic checks have to be done when an execution plan is parsed and transformed into the internal representation of the DBMS. In MIDAS a part of the routines that perform the semantic checks for SQL statements are simply reused for this task, too.

5.4.3   Parallel Evaluation

Since our parallelization approach is operator-based, we can introduce various forms of parallelism by integrating specific `send` and `receive` operators that manage data partitioning (cf. [80] and subsections 5.5.1 and 7.2.2). The parallelization can be done by the parallelizer of the DBMS itself or the developer can specify this directly within the execution plan. In any case the UDF used in the multi-operator implementation have to be registered with metadata that describes how they can be parallelized (cf. subsection 3.3.4).

5.5 Performance Evaluation

In this section, we will present initial performance measurements that indicate a significant performance increase for the evaluation of complex UDF according to the multi-operator method. Our example is a query with a spatial join, similar to the one in section 5.2.

For our measurements we have used the following environment:

- Hardware:
  We have performed our experiments using a SUN Ultra-2 workstation (model 2200) with 2 Ultra SPARC-1 processors (200 MHz each), 1MB external cache, 512 MB main memory, and 2 SUN 4 GB hard disks.
- Software:
  We have conducted our initial performance measurements using our parallel ORDBMS prototype MIDAS. MIDAS supports full intra-query parallelism on symmetric multi-processors and workstation clusters. Please refer to section 7.2 for details.
  To implement the different query execution plans for the spatial join we have used the interface described in subsection 5.4.2 and in addition defined and implemented some UDF (using an interface similar to that of commercial ORDBMS).

5.5.1   Experimental Scenario

We demonstrate the performance of the multi-operator method for the example query of section 5.2 that selects all pairs of overlapping polygons from a table with polygon geometries. We have generated random data for our experiments due to two reasons. First, this eased control over our experimental setting and second, we only wanted to demonstrate the benefits of the multi-operator method. Especially, we have not focussed on designing or evaluating special algorithms for spatial joins. Thus, using real application data seemed not to be critical to our experiments.

We have used 3 tables PG1, PG2, and PG3 that contained 1 000, 10 000 and 100 000 regular N-corners as polygons. The polygons were generated with 3 random parameters: N (the number of corner points of the polygon), the radius (distance of the corners to the center) and the location of the center in the 2 dimensional plane. The polygons of table PG2 were placed in a rectangle (our spatial universe) bounded by the points (0, 0) and (100 000, 100 000). For the table PG1 we have reduced the area of the spatial universe by a factor of 10, for table PG3 we have enlarged the area by a factor 10. Therefore, in the average the number of polygons in an area of constant size is about the same for all tables. This results in a linear growth in the number of overlapping polygon pairs in the three tables. The number of points per polygon was randomly chosen between 3 and 98 with an average of about 50. The radius was chosen as $20 + N + \lfloor r * N \rfloor$; the value r is a random number between 0 and 1. This means that the more points a polygon had, the larger was its area. Table 4 contains some statistics about the three tables. As one can see, the number of polygon pairs that actually do overlap roughly increases linearly with the cardinality of the table.

We have stored the polygon data as a list of points in a VARCHAR data type and have defined the 3 tables PG1, PG2, and PG3 that contain the polygons together with an integer value as primary key as follows:

```
CREATE TABLE PG1(INTEGER id PRIMARY KEY, VARCHAR p_geometry)
```

The tables were stored on a single disk. We have then implemented the UDF `over-laps (polygon1, polygon2)` performing a test, whether the two argument polygons overlap. The function returns an integer value of 1, if the two polygons overlap geometrically and 0 otherwise[1]. We have used the C++-library LEDA [75] for a rapid implementation of the geometric functionality.

Table 4. Statistics of the Test Data Tables

property	table PG1	table PG2	table PG3
cardinality of table	1 000	10 000	100 000
disk space (KB) [clustered in B-tree]	736	6 464	71 584
avg(# corner points / polygon):	48.35	49.97	50.01
avg(area(polygon))	31 276.7	32 689.8	32 754.3
# overlapping bounding boxes	1 188	12 144	121 460
# overlapping polygons	1 140	11 550	115 336

To avoid including the time to display the result into the measurements, we simply counted the number of result tuples. Given these explanations, our test query was simply the following, with Polygon_Table being PG1, PG2, or PG3:

```
Test Query:

SELECT    COUNT(*)
FROM      Polygon_Table AS a, Polygon_Table AS b
WHERE     overlaps(a.p_geometry, b.p_geometry) = 1
```

---

1. Boolean return type would be more appropriate, but MIDAS currently does not support this.

The first implementation of the UDF `overlaps` is straightforward: simply test whether the polygons overlap using the exact geometry (the implementation uses a (slightly modified) plane-sweeping algorithm from computational geometry provided by the library LEDA). In the following we will call this function `exact_overlaps`. Now we will explain how we have tried to speed up the evaluation of the `overlaps` predicate with the multi-operator method. This is done in several steps that are increasingly sophisticated. The first step was to use a simple filter-and-refine scheme to improve the efficiency of the implementation. The filtering step uses bounding boxes as approximations of the polygons. Bounding boxes were represented by their lower left and upper right corner coordinates and were also stored as strings. We have implemented this in the following function:

- `filter_overlaps(polygon1, polygon2)`:
  Generate and overlap bounding boxes for the input polygons first, then overlap their exact geometries, if necessary.

While `filter_overlaps` improves the performance of a single-operator implementation, it does not represent a sophisticated multi-operator implementation based on the PBSM algorithm as described in subsection 5.3.2. Thus, we implemented three additional UDF to provide suitable building blocks for the multi-operator method:

- `bbox(polygon)`:
  Create a bounding box for a given polygon.
- `bbox_overlaps(bbox1, bbox2)`:
  Test whether two bounding boxes overlap.
- `bbox_partition(bbox)`:
  Compute all buckets to which a given bounding box has to be copied.

The UDF `bbox_overlaps` does a relatively simple geometric test and is very inexpensive compared to the `exact_overlaps` function for polygons. The partitioning function `bbox_partition` divides the spatial universe in B equally sized rectangular regions that we call buckets. The function then computes all buckets, which a given bounding box overlaps. Since we divided both dimensions T times, actually B is equal to $(T+1)^2$. The actual implementation has additional parameters not shown above that define the partitioning (e.g. the value T). In Figure 20, T is 1 and B is 4.

Now we are ready to describe the four implementations of the UDP `overlaps` that we have evaluated (the implementation of the spatial join is marked in the operator graphs by the grey area)[1]:

---

1. We want to remark here that our prototype currently does not support real nested-loops joins, but is only able to perform a restriction after forming the Cartesian product. But since the execution is demand-driven and tuple-at-a-time, the intermediate Cartesian product is not materialized. In addition, MIDAS does not support OIDs. For our tests, we replaced OIDs simply by the primary key `id`.

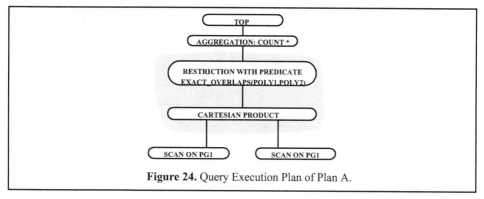

Figure 24. Query Execution Plan of Plan A.

- Plan A (naive single-operator implementation; cf. Figure 24 and Figure 23):
  Evaluate the UDF `exact_overlaps` on the Cartesian product (a × b).

- Plan B (single-operator implementation of filter-and-refine strategy; cf. Figure 25):
  Evaluate the UDF `filter_overlaps` on the Cartesian product (a × b).

- Plan C (simple multi-operator implementation; cf. Figure 26):
  Generate the bounding boxes with the UDF `bbox` for both relations a and b and store the bounding boxes of the inner relation b temporarily together with the primary key column (in Figure 26 denoted by PK). Then build the Cartesian product of the result. Evaluate the UDF `bbox_overlaps` next. For all candidate pairs - described by their primary keys (PK, PK) - retrieve the polygon data (via a B-tree) using a join on the `id` value and finally evaluate the UDF `exact_overlaps`. Altogether plan C employs four UDF: `bbox` (2x), `bbox_overlaps`, and `exact_overlaps`.

- Plan D (multi-operator implementation with spatial partitioning and merge join; cf. Figure 27):
  Plan D extends plan C by spatial partitioning for the bounding boxes. This is done by applying the user-defined partitioning function `bbox_partition` to the lower

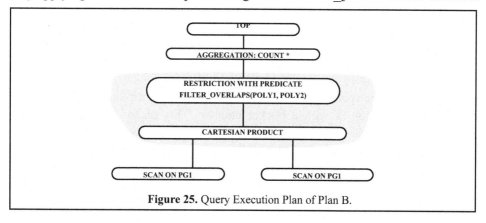

Figure 25. Query Execution Plan of Plan B.

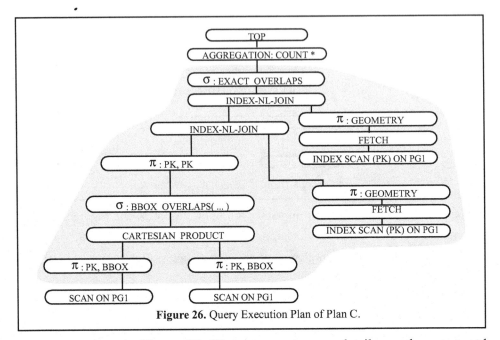

Figure 26. Query Execution Plan of Plan C.

send operators in Figure 27. We give some more details on the send and receive operators here. A send operator splits its input data stream and writes it into one or more partitions. A receive operator reads one or more data partitions and merges them into a single data stream. Usually, send and receive operators are executed by different processes. However, the send operator can optionally be executed in the same process as one of his father receive operators. Hence, if the send operator writes only into one partition then both operators can be executed by the same process, i.e., in a sequential manner. Please note that the implementation of data partitioning with user-defined partitioning functions in MIDAS also allows a partial replication. That is, if the partitioning function computes b buckets for a given tuple then this tuple is replicated b times. The effect of applying the partitioning function bbox_partition is exactly the same as that of joining a correlated table function that returns the numbers of the buckets to which a given tuple belongs. Hence, a correlated table function could be used instead of the user-defined partitioning function bbox_partition. However, correlated table functions are not available in MIDAS.

Consequently, the spatial partitioning is only a logical partitioning that is achieved by labeling the tuples with a bucket number. This means that the number of physical data partitions into which the send operator writes its output is not determined by the partitioning function. A split of the data stream into several physical data partitions is only needed for parallel execution. In this case, the topmost send and receive operator pair is needed to combine results of different partitions. As a consequence, the plan shown in Figure 27 can be executed either

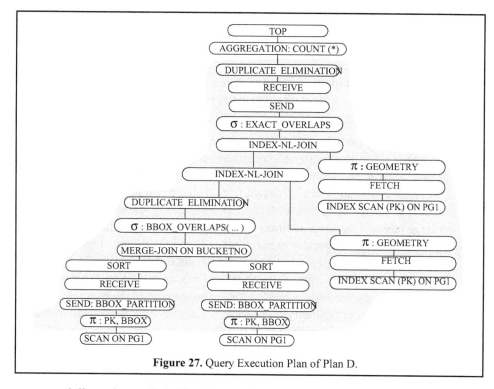

Figure 27. Query Execution Plan of Plan D.

sequentially or in parallel. The degree of parallelism is directly determined by the number of physical data partitions generated by the lower send operators which do the spatial partitioning. The number of these partitions is determined by a separate parameter of the send operator. This parameter is typically set by the parallelizer [80].

As a result of this spatial partitioning step, the bucket number is appended to each temporary tuple. This allows to join the tuples that belong to corresponding buckets using a merge join on the bucket number. Thus, the function bbox_overlaps is evaluated only on the set of all pairs of bounding boxes with the same bucket number (and not on the complete Cartesian product like in plan C). Next the elimination of duplicate candidate pairs is done and finally the UDP exact_overlaps is evaluated on the exact geometries. Altogether plan D employs six UDF: bbox (2x), bbox_partition (2x), bbox_overlaps, and exact_overlaps.

Please note that plans A and B are still traditional single-operator implementations, whereas plans C and D are multi-operator implementations. Furthermore, the quality of the UDP implementation steadily increases from the straightforward solution of plan A to the sophisticated solution of plan D, which is very similar to the redesigned PBSM algorithm (cf. subsection 5.3.2).

5.5.2 Performance Results

We present now some initial performance results. With respect to the absolute execution times, please note that we used our prototype database system and did not fine tune our UDF implementations. But the relative performance measures should give a first impression of the possible performance gains.

In Table 5, we present the sequential execution times in seconds for all plans. The last row shows the time that is needed to do the exact geometry processing for the candidate pairs (refinement). Some execution times are not available, since we did not evaluate plans with execution times higher than 100 000 seconds (nearly 28 hours). Several conclusions can be drawn from Table 5: First, there are significant performance increases for plans B, C, and D. Processing queries with expensive UDF on large tables in acceptable times obviously requires sophisticated implementations. Second, the multi-operator method (plans C and D) allows to reduce the execution time drastically. Especially, it allows to reduce the complexity of the join operation from quadratic complexity to O(N*log(N)), as can be seen for plan D. In plan D nearly all execution time is needed for the processing of the exact geometries. Given the times for exact geometry processing, we can see that the overall execution times for plans B and C still grow quadratically (i.e., they grow by a factor 100, as we move to a table that is larger by a factor of 10), if the overall execution time is dominated by the join costs. Since plan D uses spatial partitioning, the asymptotic complexity of the plan is determined by the merge join and has only a complexity of O(N *log(N)). Thus, the increase in the execution times is much slower. Since the total execution time of plan D for the test tables is dominated by the time for refinement, the overall increase of the execution time is roughly linear.

Table 5. Performance Results of Different Sequential Plans of the Test Query (Time in Seconds)

sequential execution of plan	table PG1	table PG2	table PG3
A	13582.6	not avail.	not avail.
B	430.9	41663.1	not avail.
C	50.8	3388.8	not avail.
D[a]	17.6	189.6	1908.6
D (time without refinement)	0.6	6.5	96.2
D (time for refinement only)	17.0	183.1	1812.4

a.   Please note that for plan D the results shown in Table 5 are for the spatial partitioning that yielded the lowest execution time from Table 6.

Table 6 demonstrates directly that the spatial partitioning allows to reduce the complexity of the join operation from quadratic to near linear complexity. It shows the effect of different numbers of buckets for the spatial partitioning on the number of replicated polygons and the execution time for plan D. In addition we computed the execution time minus the time for refinement. As can be seen, the execution time decreases until the number of buckets approaches the number of polygons in the table. The execution time of plan D without refinement is reduced roughly linearly with an increasing number of buckets, until the number of polygons per bucket is small. This is what we expected, as corresponding buckets are joined with a nested-loops join. Therefore, if the number of buckets is increased by a factor K, the time to join two buckets is reduced by K^2, since the number of tuples in a bucket is reduced by a factor of about K. If more buckets than polygons are used, the number of replicated polygons grows and the overall execution time goes up slightly. This is not surprising, since most of the time is needed for the exact geometry processing in these cases.

Table 6. Impact of the Number of Buckets and Replication on the Performance of Plan D (Time in Seconds)

# buckets	PG1: number of replicated polygons	PG1: exec. time for plan D	PG1: exec. time for plan D without refinement	PG 2: number of replicated polygons	PG 2: exec. time for plan D	PG 2: exec. time for plan D without refinement	PG 3: number of replicated polygons	PG3: execution time for plan D	PG3: exec. time for plan D without refinement
1	0	53.9	36.9	0	3 696.8	3 513.7	0	not avail.	not avail.
4	11	26.5	9.5	38	1 073.5	890.4	143	90 172.8	88 360.4
16	37	19.6	2.6	125	412.9	229.8	423	24 078.4	22 266.0
64	100	17.9	0.9	310	245.2	60.6	973	7 402.7	5 590.3
256	221	17.6	0.6	678	202.7	19.6	2 107	3 317.2	1 504.8
1 024	489	17.6	0.6	1 445	192.1	9.0	4 419	2 311.1	498.7
4 096	1 132	17.6	0.6	3 080	189.6	6.5	9 100	2 037.1	224.7
16 384	2 628	17.9	0.9	6 652	189.7	6.6	18 904	1 962.0	149.6
65 536	7 155	18.7	2.7	15 308	191.8	8.7	39 975	1 908.6	96.2
262 144	21 666	21.0	4.0	38 249	192.5	9.4	87 068	1 996.0	183.6

In Table 7, we present the effect of parallelism on the execution time. We executed plans B, C, and D with a degree of parallelism of 2 for the nested-loops/merge join and the restriction by `exact_overlaps`. Parallelization could be achieved as usual (cf. subsections 5.4.3 and 5.5.1, especially the description of plan D), i.e., for the nested-loops join by splitting one input into 2 partitions and by replicating the other input and for the merge join by splitting both inputs into 2 partitions using hash partitioning on the join attribute (i.e., the bucket number). Then the restriction with `exact_overlaps` was evaluated on both resulting partitions. Since the execution is always CPU-bound and we used all processors of our machine, the maximum obtainable speedup is slightly less than two, because the operating system uses some CPU resources. For sequential execution this operating system overhead can be handled by the CPU that is not used for query processing. As one can see from the speedup (shown in the shaded rows), all plans were able to profit from parallel execution, as we expected, since the execution is CPU bound. The speedup is decreasing from plan B to D, since the execution becomes less CPU-bound and I/O parallelism was not fully exploited during these tests. We did not evaluate plan A in parallel, as this plan is not usable anyway.

These initial performance results show clearly the impressive performance gains that are possible with the multi-operator method (plan D compared to the single-operator implementation plan B). In addition, the results show that parallelism can be applied to the multi-operator implementations in the usual way to speed up processing further, i.e., by means of data parallelism and pipelining.

Table 7. Performance Results for Parallel Processing of Plans B, C, and D (Time in Seconds)

plan	degree of parallelism	table PG1	table PG 2	table PG3
B	1	430.9	41 663.1	not avail.
B	2	218.6	22 129.4	not avail.
speedup	-	1.97	1.88	not avail.
C	1	50.8	3 388.8	not avail.
C	2	28.0	1 848.4	not avail.
speedup	-	1.81	1.83	not avail.
D	1	17.6	189.6	2 037.1
D	2	11.2	111.1	1 094.3
speedup	-	1.57	1.70	1.86

5.6 Related Work

User-Defined Functions (UDF) have attracted increasing interest of researchers as well as the industry in recent years (see e.g. [13], [17], [45], [47], [68], [70], [83], [89], [98], [104]). However, most of the work discusses only the non-parallel execution of UDF, special implementation techniques like caching, or it is directed towards query optimization for UDF. Patel et al. discuss in [89] support for the parallel implementation of ADT and UDF in the area of geo-spatial applications. They report that in this area complex multi-step operations are commonplace. Also special new join techniques [88] and other special implementation techniques have been proposed. However, to the best of our knowledge, there is no approach that allows the execution of such special techniques in current ORDBMS.

In [98] E-ADT (enhanced ADT) are proposed as a new approach for the architecture of ORDBMS. An ORDBMS is envisioned as a collection of E-ADT. These E-ADT encapsulate the complete functionality and implementation of the ADT. Especially all knowledge about the query language, its optimization and the execution engine are encapsulated in an E-ADT. All E-ADT implementations are linked via common interfaces. Furthermore, the implementation of new E-ADT can use a common library with base services, e.g. for storage management. We believe that this is an interesting approach that is in general more ambitious than the multi-operator method discussed here, but parallel execution is not examined for E-ADT. Basically it should be possible to use multi-operator implementations also within the E-ADT approach. While the multi-operator method might be useful for the E-ADT approach, in addition it fits very well to the architectures of current commercial ORDBMS. This is in contrast to the E-ADT approach. Therefore, the effort for ORDBMS vendors to support the multi-operator method is not too big, but its benefits are immense as reported in this chapter.

In chapter 3, we have presented techniques for the parallel execution of user-defined scalar and aggregate functions in PORDBMS. While these techniques provide some support for the parallel execution of user-defined functions that have an input context (like aggregation), the multi-operator method supports the *efficient* and parallel execution for much more user-defined functions. Therefore the multi-operator method should be seen as a further generalization and important supplementation of the previous techniques: The possibility to use several operators allows the developer to separate different parts of the implementation. This will often allow to use data parallelism for the individual parts, though a data parallel execution might not be possible for a complex single-operator implementation with external effects or a global state.

5.7 Summary

In this chapter, we proposed the multi-operator method as a new technique for the implementation of user-defined functions. The goal of this method is to provide a general implementation method that enables developers to implement efficient algorithms for complex UDPs and execute them in ORDBMS. The main advantage of the multi-operator method is that a new database operation can be implemented easily. It is only necessary to write a few UDF and place them in a database operator graph. The alternative for developers would be to write a new specialized database operator, but this is not possible in current ORDBMS. Hence, the multi-operator method is in our view a feasible and practical method that can be used without changes of the current ORDBMS core systems. The multi-operator method offers some important further advantages: the finer granularity of the implementation structure enhances *reuse, optimization,* and especially *parallelization.* The multi-operator method provides developers with a method for the implementation of complex UDPs that enables all kinds of parallelism. This support for parallel execution is a significant advantage of the multi-operator method.

An important application of the multi-operator method are user-defined join algorithms that allow highly efficient implementations of UDPs as our performance measurements have demonstrated.

In the next chapter we present a new approach to user-defined database operators and user-defined implementation rules for query optimization that in our view supersedes the multi-operator method. However, it may require a major implementation effort by ORDBMS vendors.

CHAPTER 6

User-Defined Table Operators

6.1 Introduction

Parallel database technology makes it possible to handle ever-increasing data volumes. However, this is not sufficient to process complex queries on large databases fastly. For queries that must apply complex algorithms to the data and especially for those that correlate data from several tables, it is essential to enable an efficient and completely parallel evaluation of these algorithms within the DBMS. For example, as we have shown in chapter 5, new tailored join algorithms can increase the performance for certain operations like spatial joins, etc. by orders of magnitude. But, as we have already pointed out there, it is not yet possible for third-party developers to implement efficient user-defined join algorithms in current commercial ORDBMS. In fact, one cannot implement any new database operators. UDF cannot be used to implement new operators, as they are invoked by built-in database operators. The limitation of UDTF is obvious: although they can produce an entire output table, they can only have scalar arguments. Hence, UDTF are helpful in accessing external data sources [21] etc., but cannot be used to implement new database operators like new join algorithms.

Our main contribution in this chapter is to propose a new approach to *user-defined database operators* [61]. To the best of our knowledge this is the first approach that allows third-party developers to add a new database operator to a running DBMS. The *main goals of our design* were to provide extensibility with respect to new database operators and to ensure that the design fits well to the existing technology. Especially, it should be possible to integrate the technology into current commercial ORDBMS without a major change of the system architecture. Furthermore, we considered full support for parallel execution and ease of use for developers of new operators as crucial requirements. We believe that we have met these goals.

The central new concept of our approach is to allow tables as arguments for user-defined routines and to allow the manipulation of these input tables by SQL DML commands in the body of these routines. Moreover, these routines are internally used as new database operators. One could at first expect that such an extension would

M. Jaedicke: Parallel Object-Relational Query Processing, LNCS 2169, pp. 67-105, 2001.
© Springer-Verlag Berlin Heidelberg 2001

lead to an increased complexity with respect to the development of such routines. But this is not the case, since the body of these new routines can be implemented similar to embedded SQL programs - a widely used programming concept.

The remainder of this chapter is organized as follows. Section 6.2 introduces and discusses user-defined table operators as our approach to make database systems extensible by new operators. We discuss several examples of new operators in detail in section 6.3. Finally, we discuss the related work in section 6.4 and provide our conclusions in section 6.5.

6.2 User-Defined Table Operators

If we review the current concepts for UDR from a more abstract point of view, we can observe the following: there are routines that operate on a tuple and produce a tuple (UDSF), there are routines that are invoked for each tuple of a set of tuples and produce an aggregate value (UDAF) and finally there are routines that operate on a tuple and return a table (UDTF). So obviously there is something missing: namely routines that operate on one or more tables and maybe some additional scalar parameters and can return a tuple or a table. We want to point out that the argument tables (input tables) for this kind of routines can be intermediate results of a query, that is, they are not restricted to be base tables. We call these routines *user-defined table operators* (UDTO), since they can be used to define and implement new N-ary database operators. This classification is expressed in Table 8. As one can observe, UDTO improve the orthogonality of SQL.

Table 8. A Classification of User-Defined Routines Based on their Parameter Types

		output parameter types	
		scalar	table
input parameter types	scalar	UDSF	UDTF (UDTO)
	table(s)	UDAF (UDTO)	UDTO

In the following, we will explain, how UDTO can be defined and implemented and how their processing can be integrated into parallel (object-)relational execution engines. However, we will first define a generalization relationship among row types. This will allow the application of a given UDTO to a broad range of tables, as we will see later.

6.2.1   A Generalization Relationship for Row Types

A row type $R = (R_1, R_2, ... , R_N)$ is a structured type that consists of N attributes. Each of these attributes has a data type R_i. Now we can define that a row type $S =$

$(S_1, S_2, \ldots, S_K)$ is a *subtype* of R, if $N \leq K$ and $\{R_1, R_2, \ldots, R_N\} \subseteq \{S_1, S_2, \ldots, S_K\}$. In other words, for each attribute with data type R_i of R there is some attribute with the same data type $S_j = R_i$ in S, but S may contain additional attributes with arbitrary data types. The order of the attributes in R and S is not important. We call R also *supertype* of S. Please note that each table has an associated row type.

We want to point out that this generalization relationship between subtypes is different from the supertable/subtable concept which describes a collection hierarchy and is already available in some ORDBMS [53]. As we describe in the next subsection, UDTO can be defined in such a way that they are applicable to all tables whose row type is a subtype of the row type of the formal input tables of the UDTO. Because the row type of a subtable is a subtype of the row type of the corresponding supertable, a UDTO can be applied to all subtables of a given supertable, if it is applicable to the supertable.

6.2.2   Defining and Implementing UDTO

In this subsection, we describe how UDTO can be defined and implemented based on SQL. The basic idea of this approach is easy to understand: the effect of all operators can be viewed as a mapping from a set of tables to a new table or a single tuple. This is very similar to the effect of an algebraic operator. One fundamental difference is that a user-defined operator usually does not need to have base tables as input, but tables that represent intermediate results. It also produces an intermediate result table that can be processed further. Based on these observations, we propose to implement new UDTO by means of an extended version of embedded SQL. To enable this we propose the following extensions to user-defined procedures: the definition of N input tables and a single output table for a user-defined procedure is permitted and SQL DML commands in the body of this procedure are allowed to refer to these tables. Please note that these input tables can represent intermediate results as well as base tables, table expressions, or views.

Generally speaking, a new UDTO can be executed sequentially as follows: All input tables are first materialized. That means they can furtheron be accessed in a similar way as permanently stored base tables. Then the UDTO is executed using these input tables. The UDTO produces and materializes the output table that represents the result of the UDTO and that can be processed further. Of course, the input tables cannot be manipulated and the only SQL command that is permitted for the manipulation of the output table is the INSERT command. In chapter 7 we will describe optimizations of this basic execution scheme that will allow a much more efficient execution in many cases. Moreover, we will describe how UDTO can be processed in parallel in subsection 6.2.4.

Obviously, ORDBMS must provide a statement to create UDTO. We describe the CREATE TABLE_OPERATOR statement in the syntax diagram shown in Figure 28

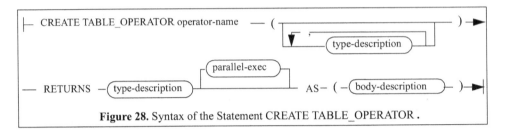

Figure 28. Syntax of the Statement CREATE TABLE_OPERATOR .

(we use | to denote beginning and end of a definition; terms in small ovals are described in additional syntax diagrams or in the text). After the name of the table operator the argument list and the return type are described. The parallel execution option allows to specify how the function can be executed in parallel (we will describe the corresponding syntax diagram in subsection 6.2.4). Finally, the body of the function follows. Please note that we have not shown other options in the syntax diagram, which are useful for other purposes like query optimization. We propose such options in the next chapter when we discuss the implementation of the UDTO concept within a DBMS.

The syntax diagram in Figure 29 presents the type description including input and output tables. Each table is described by specifying the name and data type for each column. In this syntax diagram the term 'datatype' should denote all allowed data types for columns, including user-defined types. We will explain the notation table-name.+ later.

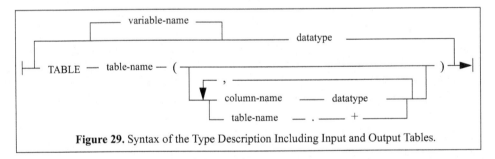

Figure 29. Syntax of the Type Description Including Input and Output Tables.

We do not provide a syntax diagram for the description of the body, because we allow here embedded SQL program code or a single INSERT statement - with some extensions of SQL. We try to use SQL/PSM as a procedural language in our examples, but our concept is not limited to a specific procedural language. That means that all procedural languages like C, C++, Java, or COBOL can be used. In addition, proprietary APIs or other techniques could be used instead of embedded SQL.

We distinguish two kinds of UDTO that differ in the implementation of their body: *procedural UDTO* and *SQL macros*. A procedural UDTO is a UDTO whose body contains procedural statements with embedded SQL statements. As for UDSF one can implement the body of a procedural UDTO in a programming language (with embedded SQL), compile it, put it into a library and register it with the DBMS. On the other hand, if the body of a UDTO consists of a single INSERT statement we call this UDTO an SQL macro. This kind of UDTO has some similarity to views, but an SQL macro can refer to the formal input tables of the UDTO and is not limited to references to base tables or views.

In the following, we present some definitions of UDTO. These examples are extremely simple and they are *not* intended to demonstrate the usefulness of the UDTO approach (cf. section 6.3 for applications). They only serve to illustrate the concept and the syntax and to introduce further details of the concept. We will refer to these examples also later in subsection 6.2.3 when we discuss the application of UDTO.

Example 1: The UDTO `minimum`

In the first example, we create a UDTO that computes the minimum for a table with an integer column:

```
CREATE TABLE_OPERATOR minimum (TABLE Input (number INTEGER))
RETURNS INTEGER
AS
{
RETURN(SELECT MIN(value) FROM Input)
};
```

This example demonstrates how a new aggregation operator can be defined. In case of aggregations, there is usually no output table, but only an aggregate value. Of course there are many aggregate functions that should be implemented as a UDAF, since this allows to compute multiple aggregates in a single pass over an input table. Hence, an implementation as a UDAF will often outperform an implementation as a UDTO in many cases.

Before we present further examples, we introduce the following extensions for the usage of SQL within the body of UDTO: First, all SQL DML statements can read the input tables in the same manner as base tables. Especially, an input table can be read by several different SQL statements. Second, tuples can be appended to the output table by INSERT commands. With these extensions, we can define our next example.

Example 2: The UDTO `has_job`

This UDTO performs a restriction of the input table and does some decoding. Let us assume that a table `employees(emp_no, job)` has been defined with an integer column `job` that is used to code the job of the employees. We assume that the names of the jobs and their code are stored in a table `jobcodes(code, jobname)`. The UDTO `has_job` reads the name for a given code from the table `jobcodes` and selects all jobs from the input table with this code. This UDTO is created as follows:

```
CREATE TABLE_OPERATOR has_job
     (TABLE Input (job INTEGER), jname VARCHAR)
RETURNS TABLE Output (job INTEGER)
AS
{
INSERT INTO Output
     SELECT I.job
     FROM Input AS I, jobcodes AS C
     WHERE I.job = C.code and C.jobname = jname
};
```

Please note that the database can be fully accessed from within the body of the UDTO. In our example the table jobcodes is accessed. This supports information hiding, since the accessed objects are not visible to the user of the UDTO. All side effects of a UDTO evaluation belong to the associated transaction. That is, the UDTO is executed within the same transaction as the statement that invokes it.

So far, UDTO can be applied reasonably only to tables that match the row types of the corresponding formal parameter tables *exactly*. For example, the UDTO has_job can be applied to a table with a single integer column. Of course, it is desirable to allow the application of a UDTO to a more general class of tables. Our goal is to allow all tables as input tables whose row types are subtypes (cf. subsection 6.2.1) of the row types of the formal UDTO input table. The UDTO operates only on columns that appear within the formal input table. All additional columns which may be present in the actual input tables are neglected or can be propagated to the output table, if this is desired (*attribute propagation*).

To support attribute propagation, developers of UDTO must be able to determine that the additional columns of an actual input table have to be appended to the output table. We denote these additional columns by the expression table_name.+ (the '+' denotes only the values of the *additional* columns. By contrast, *all* columns are usually denoted by the '*' in SQL). That means, an expression like table_name.+ has to be replaced by the values of all additional columns of the corresponding input table table_name, which are present in the actual argument table, but not in the formal argument table of the UDTO. For example, if the actual argument table that is bound to the input table input1 has one additional column, then input1.+ represents exactly the value of this column. We permit also a table variable instead of a table name in combination with '+'. Normally all additional columns of the input tables will be appended to the output table. That is, the row type of the formal output table is a supertype of the row type of the actual output table. As we will see below, these additional columns have to appear in the definition of the output table.

Now, we can redefine the UDTO has_job with attribute propagation as follows (changes are in bold face):

```
CREATE TABLE_OPERATOR has_job
     (TABLE Input (job INTEGER), jname VARCHAR)
RETURNS TABLE Output (job INTEGER, Input.+)
AS
{
INSERT INTO Output
        SELECT I.job, I.+
        FROM Input AS I, jobcodes AS C
        WHERE I.job = C.code and C.jobname = jname
};
```

As the example shows, we have to define the columns of each input table, but only those columns that are needed within the function's body should be defined. The expression I.+ appends all additional columns to the output. This allows the application of the UDTO has_job as a restriction operator, because a subset of the rows of the input table is returned. The specification of the output table contains the term Input.+ to enable type checking.

Example 3: The UDTO equal

Finally, we present an equi-join as new operator equal:

```
CREATE TABLE_OPERATOR equal(TABLE Input1(value1 INTEGER),
                    TABLE Input2(value2 INTEGER))
RETURNS  TABLE  Output  (value1  INTEGER,  Input1.+,  value2  INTEGER,
Input2.+)
AS
{
    INSERT INTO Output
        SELECT value1, Input1.+, value2, Input2.+
        FROM Input1, Input2
        WHERE Input1.value1 = Input2.value2
};
```

The UDTO equal can now be applied to join all tables with a column of type integer. This UDTO, same as the other examples, is an SQL macro.

Row Identification

Finally, we want to propose an extension that allows to implement UDTO more efficiently. Within the body of a UDTO it can be necessary to have access to a unique identifier for each row of an input table (cf. subsection 6.3.1 for an example). To support this, we introduce the special column data type ID for the type description of table columns that are UDTO arguments. The special type ID means that the column contains a unique identifier for each row of an input table. Note that an ID can be either a primary key or an internal identifier like a row identifier or a reference type as proposed in SQL3. Such an ID can always be generated automatically by the DBMS (this can be viewed as a kind of type promotion for row types). An ID column could also be created explicitly in the body of the UDTO by the developer, but, if it is defined as a column of an input table, the DBMS can use an already existing identifier as an optimization. In general, it is not useful to append a column value of type ID explicitly to the output table. In case the primary key is used internally to represent the ID, the system does this automatically, if the '+' option has been specified in the projection list of the subquery of the INSERT statement.

6.2.3   The Different Usages of the UDTO Concept

In this subsection, we will describe two ways in which UDTO can be applied: first they can be used explicitly by programmers within SQL commands. This allows to extend the functionality of SQL in arbitrary ways and it allows to use UDTO to enhance the performance in special situations (that the query optimizer might not be able to detect and optimize appropriately). Second, UDTO can additionally be used as new implementation methods for query execution plans. In this case, the query optimizer employs the UDTO during the plan generation whenever the use of this UDTO leads to a cheaper query execution plan. This is especially useful to provide more efficient implementations of UDF. We discuss these two applications now in more detail.

Augmentation of SQL through the Explicit Usage of UDTO

UDTO can be used explicitly in SQL statements by programmers. This allows to extend the functionality of SQL by arbitrary new set operations or to say it in other words: UDTO make object-relational query processing universal in the sense that the set of database operations becomes extensible. For example, over time a lot of special join operations were proposed: cross join, inner join, anti-join, left, right, and full outer join, union join, etc. Moreover, other operations like recursion or more application-specific ones (for data mining, etc.) have been introduced. UDTO allow developers to define a parallelizable implementation for such operators. These operators can then be invoked in SQL commands by application programmers, as we explain in the following.

A UDTO that returns a table can be used in all places within SQL commands where a table expression is allowed. Moreover, UDTO with two input tables can be written in infix notation to allow an easy integration into the current SQL command syntax. For example, one could define a UDTO named ANTI_JOIN. Then one can write the following expression in the FROM clause: Table1 ANTI_JOIN Table2. Seen from a conceptual point of view, in this case the Cartesian product of the output table of the UDTO and of all other tables, views, and table expressions in the FROM clause is computed. In addition, UDTO can also be written in infix notation between two SELECT blocks like the usual set operations (UNION, INTERSECT, EXCEPT).

To allow the application of UDTO to base tables and views whose row type is a subtype of the row type of the formal input table, we propose the following syntax to bind columns of the actual input table to columns of the formal input table. The programmer can specify an ordered list of columns from a given table (or view) that is bound to the corresponding columns in the parameter list of the UDTO. For example, the expression TO1 (T1 USING (C_1, C_2, ..., C_N)) describes that the columns named C_1, C_2, ..., C_N of table T1 are bound to the N columns of the formal input table parameter of the UDTO TO1. The keyword USING is optional and can be skipped. This notation can also be used, if binary UDTO are written in infix notation (it can be seen as a generalization of the ON clause for traditional join expressions). If input tables are given as table expressions then the columns of the resulting table are bound to the columns of the formal input table in exactly the order in which these columns appear in the SELECT clause of the table expression.

The following statements illustrate this syntax. They invoke the UDTO has_job explicitly with a base table and a table expression:

```
SELECT *
FROM has_job(employees USING (job), 'manager')

SELECT *
FROM has_job( (SELECT job, emp_no FROM employees), 'manager')
```

UDTO as an Augmentation of the Implementation of UDF

Next, we describe how UDTO can be used to improve the performance for queries with UDF. A very important usage of UDTO is to provide more efficient operators that can be used by the query optimizer during the plan generation. While there might be many relational queries that can be enhanced by UDTO, the move to object-relational query processing with UDF creates a need for UDTO as we have already outlined in section 5.2. The reason is that UDTO allow to implement database operations that involve UDF sometimes more efficiently than in current ORDBMS, where a built-in database operator invokes the UDF.

UDTO provide a different implementation technique for operations involving UDF compared to the traditional approach for UDF implementation. For example, a UDSF can be used as a UDP in a *join*, i.e., in a restriction involving attributes from different tables on top of a Cartesian product. In this case, a UDTO will often allow a more efficient implementation. The reason is that in current ORDBMS, the UDP is evaluated by a nested-loops join operator which has quadratic complexity. By contrast, there might exist implementation methods with much lower complexity. Therefore joins are an important application of UDTO, where performance enhancements of orders of magnitude are possible (often because nested-loops joins can be replaced by hash- or sort-merge-based join algorithms; cf. subsection 6.3.1).

Furthermore, UDTO might sometimes be useful as aggregation, restriction, or projection operators. For example, in case of UDAF it can be useful to provide an implementation by means of a UDTO, since this allows access to the whole input column for the aggregation (cf. subsection 6.3.3 for an example).

The query optimizer must decide when a UDTO should be used. In a rule-based query optimizer ([30], [36], [67]) this means the following: there must be a rule that generates a plan with the UDTO as an alternative implementation. Such a rule has to be specified by the developer. This is not difficult in this scenario, because the UDTO is always associated with a specific UDF for which it implements a specific database operator (for example, a join that has exactly this UDF as join predicate). Hence, the developer must tell the query optimizer only that the UDTO can be used to evaluate the UDF. For this purpose, the CREATE FUNCTION statement used to register UDF with the DBMS can be extended. The statement should include the option to specify that a UDTO can be used as an implementation for a specific operation such as a join. For example, one could extend the CREATE FUNCTION statement as follows:

```
ALLOW <UDTO-name> AS
(JOIN | RESTRICTION | PROJECTION | AGGREGATION) OPERATOR
```

The relationship between the UDF and the UDTO is stored in the system tables and can be used by the query optimizer. The query optimizer has to be extended by general rules that can perform these transformations for arbitrary UDF. The optimizer uses information from the system tables to decide whether the transformation is possible for a given UDF. Please note that for some functions like a UDAF, the UDTO might be the only implementation. In this case, the UDF must be executed by means of the UDTO.

Let us assume that we want to create two UDPs has_job and equal for the UDTO that we have introduced in subsection 6.2.2. Then one can register the UDP has_job with the UDTO has_job as restriction operator and the UDP equal with the UDTO equal as join operator:

```
CREATE FUNCTION has_job (INTEGER, VARCHAR) RETURNS BOOLEAN
        ALLOW has_job AS RESTRICTION OPERATOR ...

CREATE FUNCTION equal (INTEGER, INTEGER) RETURNS BOOLEAN
        ALLOW equal AS JOIN OPERATOR ...
```

Then the query optimizer considers the UDTO has_job as an implementation for the restriction with the UDP has_job in the following query:

```
SELECT *
FROM employees AS E
WHERE has_job(E.job, 'manager')
```

The same holds with respect to equal in the query:

```
SELECT *
FROM projects AS P, employees AS E
WHERE equal(E.emp_no, P.mgr_no)
```

If the application of the UDTO equal is properly optimized, the latter statement will have exactly the same query execution plan as the query:

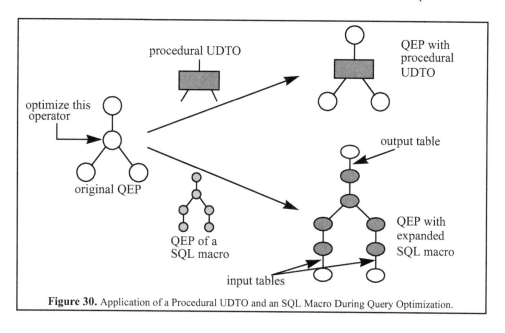

Figure 30. Application of a Procedural UDTO and an SQL Macro During Query Optimization.

```
SELECT *
FROM projects AS P, employees AS E
WHERE E.emp_no = P.mgr_no
```

Figure 30 illustrates how a traditional database operator that invokes a UDF is replaced by a UDTO. First the operator has to be identified in the original query execution plan (QEP). Then the optimizer replaces this operator either by a procedural UDTO or by an SQL macro. Because the body of an SQL macro consists essentially of a QEP we can simply replace the operator by this QEP (*SQL macro expansion*). However the QEP of the SQL macro has to be modified so that it fits to the comprising QEP. For example, proper attribute propagation has to be considered. The result of this SQL macro expansion is a traditional QEP, which can be further optimized and evaluated as usual. Especially, no materialization of input and output tables is necessary.

We close this subsection with the remark that the application of procedural UDTO to UPDATE and DELETE commands is permitted only, if proper identification of output tuples to input tuples is given. This is necessary in the case that tuples of the output table are used to identify tuples that must be modified.

6.2.4   Parallel Processing of Procedural UDTO

Nowadays new operators would not be a concept of great use, if these operators could not be executed in parallel. That is why we will discuss the parallel execution of new UDTO in this subsection. Please note that all SQL DML commands within the body of UDTO of the implementation are parallelizable as usual. If the UDTO is an SQL macro that is a single SQL statement, the complete UDTO can be parallelized automatically by the DBMS. In the more general case of a UDTO that is implemented by embedded SQL, the developer must specify how a parallel execution can be done, if it is possible at all.

We provide a method that allows to specify, if an operator can be executed with data parallelism and, should the occasion arise, how the operator can be processed. Applying data parallelism means that one or more of the input tables of an operator are split horizontally in several partitions by means of a suitable partitioning function. We demand that all input tables that have to be partitioned are split into the same number of partitions. If one or more, but not all input tables can be partitioned, the other input tables are replicated. Then the operator is executed once for each partition with the following input tables: if the argument table is partitionable, the respective partition of this table is used. If the argument table is not partitionable, then the complete replicated table is used as an argument. As a consequence, if one or more input tables are split into N partitions, then N instances of the operator are executed in parallel. Hence, the degree of parallelism is N. In this case, the final result is computed by combining the N intermediate output tables by means of a union (without elimination of duplicates). If no input table is partitioned the operator is executed without data parallelism - that is sequentially. There can be several options for the parallelization of an operator, depending on which input tables are partitioned and depending on how this partitioning is done.

Hence, we must describe the set of all combinations of partitioning functions that can be used to partition the input tables of a given UDTO. We permit different partitioning functions for different tables, but all partitioned input tables must have the same number of partitions. Therefore the partitioning functions must have a parameter that allows to specify the number of generated partitions. This parameter enables the optimizer to set the degree of parallelism for a given UDTO. In some cases, it may be also necessary to specify that exactly the same partitioning function has to be used for some or all input tables. For example, this is needed for equi-joins in relational processing.

In chapter 3 we have already proposed the following classes of partitioning functions: ANY, EQUAL and RANGE. In addition to these three partitioning classes we have proposed that a special user-defined partitioning function can be specified, too. Based on these considerations we have developed the parallel execution option in the CREATE TABLE_OPERATOR statement that allows to specify *all* parallel execution schemes which are possible for a new operator. For operators having multiple input tables many options are conceivable. But since we doubt that there will be many complex operators with more than two input tables in practice, we have not tried to optimize the description for this special case. Figure 31 shows the syntax diagram for this option.

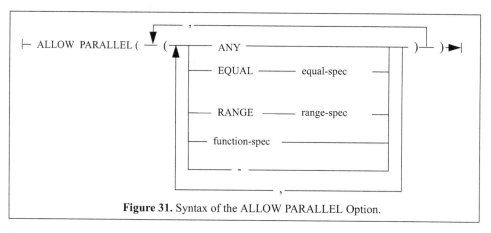

Figure 31. Syntax of the ALLOW PARALLEL Option.

If the partitioning class is not ANY, we have to specify the columns to which the partitioning function should be applied. The same is necessary, if a specific partitioning function must be used. We have left out these details in the syntax diagram. If no partitioning is possible for a given input table, this is denoted by '-' (in case of parallel processing, this input table is replicated).

In the following, we will describe some examples of parallel execution schemes for familiar (relational) operations: a restriction, a nested-loops join, a hash join and a merge join. To simplify the examples, we have left out the column specifications of the input and the output tables and the bodies of the operators.

```
CREATE TABLE_OPERATOR restriction(TABLE Input1(..))
RETURNS TABLE Output1(...)
ALLOW PARALLEL ((ANY))
AS { ... };
```

Because the class ANY is specified in the ALLOW PARALLEL option of the UDTO restriction all partitioning functions can be used to partition the input table for the restriction operator which is defined in this example.

```
CREATE TABLE_OPERATOR nested_loops(TABLE Input1(...), TABLE Input2(...))
RETURNS TABLE Output1(...)
ALLOW PARALLEL ((ANY,-), (-,ANY))
AS { ... };
```

```
CREATE TABLE_OPERATOR hash_join(TABLE Input1(...), TABLE Input2(...))
RETURNS TABLE Output1(...)
ALLOW PARALLEL ((EQUAL pf1(Column_List), EQUAL pf1(Column_List)),
          (ANY,-), (-,ANY))
AS { ... };
```

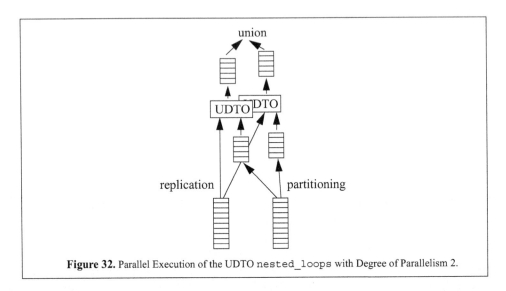

Figure 32. Parallel Execution of the UDTO `nested_loops` with Degree of Parallelism 2.

```
CREATE TABLE_OPERATOR merge_join(TABLE Input1(...), TABLE Input2(...))
RETURNS TABLE Output1(...)
ALLOW PARALLEL ((EQUAL pf1(Column_List), EQUAL pf1(Column_List)),
        (ANY,-), (-,ANY))
AS { ... };
```

The options for the three join algorithms specify that if one table is replicated, the other table can be partitioned with any partitioning function. Figure 32 illustrates data partitioning and parallel execution for the UDTO nested_loops with degree of parallelism 2. In addition, the hash join can be parallelized with the partitioning scheme (EQUAL pf1(Column_List), EQUAL pf1(Column_List)) that means both input tables are partitioned with the *same* partitioning function pf1. The same holds for the merge join, if we restrict it to the computation of equi-joins. If we want to use the merge join for more general join predicates - for example an interval join (to execute a predicate like 'x <= y + k or x >= y - k' more efficiently) - then we need a partitioning with a function of class RANGE(k), that is, the option should be ALLOW PARALLEL (RANGE(k) pf1(Column_List), RANGE(k) pf1(Column_List)). The parameter k could be an argument of this join operator (the corresponding UDP would be used as follows: interval_join(table1.x, table2.y, k)).

6.2.5   Extension to Multiple Output Tables

We can provide even more extensibility, if we allow multiple output tables for UDTO: one application could be to return a set of tables perhaps holding complex objects that are linked via OIDs. This is something like pushing Starburst's XNF

([74], [93]) into the middle of SQL commands. Using such a UDTO at the top of a query would allow for composite objects as a result. Internally, the top operator of queries has to be extended to allow the direct output of several tables as a result of a query. Another use of multiple output tables could be to support a nesting of complex UDTO. The output tables of one UDTO can then serve as input tables for other UDTO.

UDTO with multiple output tables can be used within the FROM clause of queries but not in the WHERE clause, since they do not return a table expression. The renaming of the result tables and their columns should be allowed. UDTO with multiple output tables can be evaluated in the same manner as UDTO with a single output table, but they produce multiple output tables. These output tables can be processed further. The result tables in case of a parallel evaluation are obtained by a union of all corresponding partial result tables.

6.3 Example Applications for UDTO

In this section, we will describe several examples of UDTO in order to demonstrate the broad applicability with regard to the implementation of complex operations in different processing scenarios. We present joins and restrictions for spatial data, complex aggregations and data transformations and association rule mining as examples. Some examples contain additional material or show further benefits of the UDTO concept.

6.3.1   Computing a Spatial Join

In our first example we use the UDTO concept to define a spatial join based on the partition-based spatial-merge join (PBSM) algorithm [88]. Thus, we show that the UDTO concept allows among other things a much more elegant implementation than the multi-operator method, which we have demonstrated using the same example scenario in chapter 5. Let us briefly recall this scenario. We consider the following polygon intersection query (that searches for all gold deposits intersecting lakes) as a concrete example of a spatial join:

```
SELECT    *
FROM      Lakes as L, Gold_Deposits as G
WHERE     overlaps(L.poly_geometry, G.poly_geometry)
```

The predicate `overlaps (polygon, polygon)` returns TRUE, if the two polygons overlap geometrically and FALSE otherwise. In order to define a UDTO for `overlaps` based on the PBSM algorithm we create some UDF introduced in subsection 5.5.1 for the multi-operator implementation:

- `bbox(polygon)`:
  This UDSF creates and returns the minimum bounding rectangle for a given polygon.

- `bbox_overlaps(bbox1, bbox2)`:
  This UDP returns true, if the two bounding boxes overlap.

- `exact_overlaps(polygon1, polygon2)`:
  This UDP returns true, if the exact geometries of the input polygons overlap.

- `bucket_no(bbox)`:
  This UDTF divides the spatial universe into B equally sized rectangular regions called buckets. Then it computes and returns all buckets, which the input bounding box intersects. Please note that this is a table function, that is, it returns a table with a single column of type integer.

With these UDF we are prepared to create the UDTO `overlaps`. This operator uses three techniques to improve the efficiency of the join algorithm. First, it uses a simple filter-and-refine scheme [87]. The filtering step uses bounding boxes as approximations of the polygons. This means that we test whether the bounding boxes overlap, before we check whether the exact geometries overlap. Second, spatial partitioning is used. This allows to join only the corresponding buckets. Third, the exact geometry is eliminated to reduce the data volumes of the input tables of the join. For the refinement the exact geometry is retrieved. This results in the following implementation of the overlaps predicate by means of a new join operator:

```
CREATE TABLE_OPERATOR overlaps(TABLE Input1(id1 ID, poly1 POLYGON),
          TABLE Input2(id2 ID, poly2 POLYGON))
RETURNS  TABLE  Output1(poly1  POLYGON,  Input1.+,  poly2  POLYGON,
Input2.+)
AS
{
INSERT INTO Output1
WITH    Temp1(id, bbox, bucket) AS
        (SELECT id1, bbox(poly1), bucket
         FROM Input1, TABLE (bucket_no(bbox(poly1))) AS B(bucket)),
        Temp2(id, bbox, bucket) AS
        (SELECT id2, bbox(poly2), bucket
         FROM Input2, TABLE (bucket_no(bbox(poly2))) AS B(bucket))

SELECT poly1, Input1.+, poly2, Input2.+

FROM    (SELECT DISTINCT Temp1.id AS id1, Temp2.id AS id2
         FROM Temp1, Temp2
         WHERE Temp1.bucket = Temp2.bucket AND
               bbox_overlaps(Temp1.bbox, Temp2.bbox)) AS Temp3,
        Input1, Input2

WHERE   Temp3.id1 = Input1.id1 AND
        Temp3.id2 = Input2.id2 AND
        exact_overlaps(Input1.poly1, Input2.poly2)
};
```

```
CREATE FUNCTION overlaps (POLYGON, POLYGON) RETURNS BOOLEAN
     ALLOW overlaps AS JOIN OPERATOR ...
```

As one can observe, this SQL macro allows a very readable representation of the algorithm (at least if one is experienced with SQL). The subqueries in the WITH clause generate two temporary tables with the bounding boxes and the bucket numbers for spatial partitioning. Since the UDTF bucket_no is used in the FROM clause with a correlated tuple variable, the Cartesian product with the corresponding tuple is generated. That is, we replicate the tuple for each intersecting bucket and append the bucket number (a single polygon can intersect several buckets [88]). This allows later on to join the temporary tables on the bucket number (Temp1.bucket = Temp2.bucket in the innermost SELECT query). Hence, the function bbox_overlaps is only evaluated on the Cartesian product of all polygons within the same bucket. Next, duplicate candidate pairs, which might have been introduced by the spatial partitioning, are eliminated. Finally, in the outermost SELECT statement, the UDF exact_overlaps is processed on the exact polygon geometries that are fetched from the input tables using an equi-join on the unique values of the ID columns.

We want to add some remarks concerning this example. The UDTO overlaps is an SQL macro and can be parallelized automatically. Thus, there is no need to specify an option for parallel execution. In order to process the join with data parallelism the bucket number would be selected as a partitioning column due to the equi-join on the bucket number. Therefore no specific user-defined partitioning function is needed for parallel processing, as the usual partitioning functions can be applied to the bucket number, which is an integer value. Please note that if the join on the bucket number is done via a hash join with linear complexity, the overall complexity of the UDTO is still linear. This is *much* better than the quadratic complexity of the Cartesian product that has to be used, if no UDTO is provided. In subsection 5.5.2 we have evaluated an implementation of a spatial join with a similar execution plan (plan D). Our measurements have demonstrated that this approach leads to performance gains of orders of magnitude compared to current technology and makes parallel processing of the join possible. We present a brief evaluation of the implementation with an SQL macro later in subsection 7.7.1.

A final, but important point concerns the function bucket_no which computes a spatial partitioning. Actually this function is too simple for applications. The reason is that it is crucial for the performance of the algorithm to find a suitable partitioning of the spatial universe as our measurements in subsection 5.5.2 have demonstrated. The spatial universe is the area which contains all polygons from both relations. The task is to find a suitable partitioning of the spatial universe into buckets such that each bucket contains roughly the same number of polygons (or at least the number of polygons per bucket should not vary extremely). This task is difficult, because it should ideally take the following parameters into account: the number of polygons in each input table, their spatial location, their area, the number of points per polygon and their spatial distribution. For traditional relational queries the optimizer tries to use more or less sophisticated statistics that are stored in the system tables to estimate value distributions, etc. In the same manner one could now use such metadata from (user-defined) system tables to compute parameters for the spatial partitioning. However, the fundamental problem with this approach is that the input tables do not correspond to base relations and may have therefore different value distributions (furthermore, the statistics might not be up to date). A more sophisticated approach would be to analyze the polygons in the input tables by extracting statistics about the bounding boxes and to use these statistics to derive an appropriate spatial partitioning. UDTO provide full support for this method as we will show below. Therefore UDTO support *run-time optimization* taking the actual contents of the input tables into account.

A More Sophisticated Spatial Partitioning Step

In the following, we propose a more sophisticated version of the spatial join with an enhanced user-defined data partitioning. We assume here that the polygons are roughly uniformly distributed in the spatial universe and therefore partition the space into rectangular buckets of the same size. If a polygon overlaps several buckets, the function bucket_no returns the numbers of all these buckets. We analyze the input data in the following way: We first compute the coordinates of the (rectangular) spatial universe using functions like x_lower that extract the lower x-coordinate from a bounding box and the overall number of polygons and pass these values as parameters to the UDF bucket_no. This function divides the spatial universe into buckets in such a way that each bucket holds roughly 10 polygons. The value 10 - being a constant in the function bucket_no - is chosen as a heuristic (cf. subsection 5.5.2) that will not always yield the highest performance. However, it should lead to a good performance in many situations. An improved version of the UDTO overlaps that demonstrates this method is shown below:

```
CREATE TABLE_OPERATOR overlaps(TABLE Input1(id1 ID, poly1 POLYGON),
                TABLE Input2(id2 ID, poly2 POLYGON))
RETURNS TABLE Output1(poly1 POLYGON, Input1.+, poly2 POLYGON, Input2.+)
AS
{
INSERT INTO Output1
WITH NEW1 (ID, bbox) AS
     (SELECT ID1, bbox(poly1) FROM Input1)
     NEW2 (ID, bbox) AS
     (SELECT ID2, bbox(poly2) FROM Input2)
     NEW3 (XMIN, YMIN, XMAX, YMAX, CARD) AS
     (SELECT MIN(xmin1), MIN(ymin1), MAX(xmax1), MAX(ymax1), SUM(card1)
      FROM        (SELECT  MIN(x_lower(bbox)) AS xmin1,
                           MIN(y_lower(bbox)) AS ymin1,
                           MAX (x_upper(bbox)) AS xmax1,
                           MAX (y_upper(bbox)) AS ymax1,
                           COUNT(*) AS card1
```

```
                 FROM NEW1
                 UNION
                 SELECT   MIN(x_lower(bbox)) AS xmin1,
                          MIN(y_lower(bbox)) AS ymin1,
                          MAX (x_upper(bbox)) AS xmax1,
                          MAX (y_upper(bbox)) AS ymax1,
                          COUNT(*) AS card1
                 FROM NEW2)),
      Temp1(ID, bbox, bucket) AS
      (SELECT ID, bbox, bucket
       FROM NEW1, NEW3, TABLE (bucket_no(bbox, XMIN, XMAX, YMIN,
                          YMAX, CARD)) AS B(bucket)),
      Temp2(ID, bbox, bucket) AS
      (SELECT ID, bbox, bucket
       FROM NEW2, NEW3, TABLE (bucket_no(bbox, XMIN, XMAX, YMIN,
                          YMAX, CARD)) AS B(bucket))

  SELECT poly1, Input1.+, poly2, Input2.+

  FROM (SELECT DISTINCT Temp1.id AS id1, Temp2.id AS id2
        FROM Temp1, Temp2
        WHERE Temp1.bucket = Temp2.bucket AND
              bbox_overlaps(Temp1.bbox, Temp2.bbox)) AS Temp3,
        Input1, Input2

  WHERE Temp3.id1 = Input1.id1 AND
        Temp3.id2 = Input2.id2 AND
        exact_overlaps(Input1.poly1, Input2.poly2)
  };
```

In addition to the previous algorithm this one computes the table NEW3 that contains the statistics for the data in the input tables. Then these statistics are used to derive the tables Temp1 and Temp2. The remainder of the algorithm is the same as in the previous algorithm.

6.3.2   Different UDTO for the Same Predicate

In this subsection, we would like to discuss the spatial predicate distance_less_than that checks whether the distance between two points is less than a given maximum distance. We define a UDT POINT for points in a 2-dimensional plane with appropriate UDF like x() and y() that return the coordinates of a point. For example, in the following query we would like to find all IT businesses located within 50 km of a university. In our example, columns with the name location have always the data type POINT:

Statement 1:

```
SELECT U.name, B.name
FROM universities U, businesses B
WHERE   B.type = 'IT'
        AND distance_less_than(U.location,B.location,50)
```

In this query the predicate `distance_less_than` is used as a join predicate like the overlaps predicate in the previous subsection. However, the predicate could also be used as a restriction as in the following example where we want to find only IT businesses near the given location (10, 40) that may represent a specific university:

Statement 2:

```
SELECT  B.name
FROM    businesses B
WHERE   B.type = 'IT' AND distance_less_than(B.location, point(10,40), 50)
```

In general, the different operations in which a UDP can be evaluated depend on its actual use within the QEP of a given SQL statement. In the following we will discuss these different operations and demonstrate how we can employ UDTO as more efficient implementations. Because we will define UDTO only as SQL macros, we can view this approach also as a way to write new rules for an extensible query optimizer. However, no new rules are created. We create only *new instances of generic optimization rules for UDPs*. We will discuss query optimization in the next chapter in more detail.

Obviously we can distinguish between different operations based on the type of the parameters of the corresponding UDP `distance_less_than`. The first and the second parameter can be constant values or they can be attribute values from a tuple. Moreover, the tuples can come from a single table or from two tables. Hence, we can define the following UDTO that have a different signature and are discussed below in detail:

```
CREATE TABLE_OPERATOR distance_restriction_1
(TABLE Input (p₁ POINT), p₂ POINT, maxdist DOUBLE)
RETURNS
TABLE Output (p₁ POINT, Input.+)
AS
INSERT INTO Output
SELECT p₁, I.+
FROM Input AS I
WHERE internal_distance_less_than(p₁, p₂, maxdist)
      AND contains(buffer(p₂, maxdist), p₁)


CREATE TABLE_OPERATOR distance_restriction_2
(p₁ POINT, TABLE Input (p₂ POINT), maxdist DOUBLE)
RETURNS
TABLE Output (p₂ POINT, Input.+)
AS
INSERT INTO Output
SELECT p₂, I.+
FROM Input AS I
WHERE internal_distance_less_than(p₁, p₂, maxdist)
      AND contains(buffer(p₁, maxdist), p₂)
```

```
CREATE TABLE_OPERATOR distance_restriction_3
(TABLE Input (p₁ POINT, p₂ POINT), maxdist DOUBLE)
RETURNS
TABLE Output (p₁ POINT, p₂ POINT, Input.+)
AS
INSERT INTO Output
SELECT p₁, p₂, I.+
FROM Input AS I
WHERE internal_distance_less_than(p₁, p₂, maxdist)


CREATE TABLE_OPERATOR distance_join_1
(TABLE Input₁ (p₁ POINT), TABLE Input₂ (p₂ POINT), maxdist DOUBLE)
RETURNS
TABLE Output (p₁ POINT, Input₁.+, p₂ POINT, Input₂.+)
AS
INSERT INTO Output
SELECT p₁, I₁.+, p₂, I₂.+
FROM Input₁ AS I₁, Input₂ AS I₂
WHERE internal_distance_less_than(p₁, p₂, maxdist)
      AND contains(buffer(p₂, maxdist), p₁)


CREATE TABLE_OPERATOR distance_join_2
(TABLE Input₁ (p₁ POINT), TABLE Input₂ (p₂ POINT), maxdist DOUBLE)
RETURNS
TABLE Output (p₁ POINT, Input₁.+, p₂ POINT, Input₂.+)
AS
INSERT INTO Output
SELECT p₁, I₁.+, p₂, I₂.+
FROM Input₁ AS I₁, Input₂ AS I₂
WHERE internal_distance_less_than(p₁, p₂, maxdist)
      AND contains(buffer(p₁, maxdist), p₂)


CREATE FUNCTION distance_less_than (POINT, POINT, DOUBLE)
RETURNS BOOLEAN
ALLOW distance_join_1, distance_join_2 AS JOIN OPERATOR
ALLOW distance_restriction_1, distance_restriction_2,
      distance_restriction_3 AS RESTRICTION OPERATOR
```

Let us now discuss the different UDTO. The first three UDTO are used for restriction operations. The UDTO, distance_restriction_1 and distance_restriction_2, have symmetric definitions. In their body we have used two UDSF: contains and buffer. The function buffer (point, distance) generates a box with the point as center and sides with length 2*distance. Then the function contains(box,point) is used to test if the point is contained within the box. In general, a restriction with such an additional predicate is more expensive than the evaluation of the original UDP (that has the same implementation as the function internal_distance_less_than). However, if there is a spatial index on the input table that can be used to evaluate the predicate contains, a performance enhancement of orders of magnitude can be achieved because a full table scan is replaced by an index access which typically selects only a tiny fraction of the table. It is the task of a cost-based optimizer to decide which of the two implementations, a restriction with the original UDP or the UDTO, is more efficient for a given query. The registration of a UDTO as a restriction operation simply tells the query optimizer that a second implementation method is available.

Finally, there is the case that both points are contained in the same table. This can happen, if a restriction on a base table is specified, or if several join predicates exist between two tables. In the latter case only one join predicate can be evaluated by a join operator and the others have to be evaluated on the result. The UDTO `distance_restriction_3` is trivial, since it seems to be difficult to enhance such operations. The only technique that we can imagine, is predicate caching [47]. In practice one would not define a UDTO for this kind of restriction operation. Please note that in this example the optimizer has to select one of the three UDTO for the restriction based on their signature. In addition, different implementations with the same signature may exist, as we will discuss below.

The last UDTO, `distance_join_1` and `distance_join_2`, may be applied as an alternative implementation for a join between two tables when `distance_less_than` is used as a join predicate. Of course, other implementation methods are possible and we could register several UDTO as alternative join methods (for example methods that use spatial partitioning similar to the UDTO for the predicate `overlaps` in the previous subsection). These two UDTO are useful, if there is a spatial index on the points of an input table that can be used to evaluate the `contains` predicate. In this case, an index-nested-loops join can be used instead of a nested-loops join. The optimizer will then generate alternative execution plans using both UDTO, if appropriate. Because these alternatives have an additional predicate, they will be only selected if the `contains` predicate can be evaluated using an index nested-loops join. This is cheaper than the evaluation of the predicate `distance_less_than` by a nested-loops join.

One could add the following pseudo UDTO that describes the case that no table is involved:

```
CREATE TABLE_OPERATOR distance_scalar_function
(p₁ POINT, p₂ POINT, maxdist DOUBLE)
RETURNS BOOLEAN
AS
RETURN(internal_distance_less_than(p₁,p₂,maxdist))
```

Of course this is not a correct UDTO, because we have no input table. However, this pseudo UDTO represents the case that is always reasonably implemented as a UDSF. Since no input table is involved, it is not possible to improve the efficiency by a UDTO.

This example shows clearly two points: first, it is beneficial to study the different operations in which a UDP can be evaluated. UDTO allow to describe these different scenarios in an adequate syntax. Second, it can be beneficial to provide one or more UDTO as alternative high-performance implementations for these different operations. This allows to make use of indexes as well as special algorithms and data structures.

6.3.3   Computing the Median: An Aggregation Operator

In this section, we will reconsider the aggregate function median (cf. subsection 3.4.3) as a complex aggregation operation and show that it can be implemented in a clean and efficient way as a procedural UDTO.

```
            SELECT Median(P.Age)
            FROM Persons AS P
```

Figure 33. Computing the Median by Means of a UDTO.

As in subsection 3.4.3 let us assume that we want to select the median of the ages of certain persons. The corresponding query with the UDAF Median is shown in Figure 33. In contrast to the query in subsection 3.4.3 (Figure 12) we do not need to pass the count of the input table explicitly to the median operator and hence do not need to nest aggregation operations. The reason is that we can implement the counting step within the body of the UDTO. In the UDTO the position of the median is first determined by counting the input table. Then the input table is sorted and the median is computed by fetching values from the sorted table, until the correct position is reached. Here are the statements to create the UDTO median and the corresponding UDAF:

```
CREATE TABLE_OPERATOR median (TABLE Input1(value INTEGER))
RETURNS INTEGER
AS
{
        DECLARE count, cardinality, median_pos, result INTEGER;
        SET count = 1;
        SELECT COUNT(*) FROM Input1 INTO cardinality;
        SET median_pos = ceiling ((cardinality + 1) / 2);
    F1: FOR result AS SELECT * FROM Input1 ORDER BY value ASC
        DO
            IF (count = median_pos) THEN
                  LEAVE F1;
            SET count = count + 1;
        END FOR;
        RETURN result;
};

CREATE AGGREGATE Median (INTEGER) RETURNS INTEGER
        ALLOW median AS AGGREGATION OPERATOR ...
```

This example demonstrates how SQL DML statements and procedural statements can be mixed in the body of a UDTO. While this implementation does not use the most efficient algorithm known to compute the median, the algorithm is easy to implement based on SQL and allows a computation for arbitrary large data sets, as it does not rely on explicit intermediate data storage in main memory. Moreover, both embedded SQL queries can be evaluated in parallel as usual. That means that the optimizer can automatically decide to perform the sort operation for the ORDER BY clause in parallel. Moreover, if the input table has already the required sort order, the sort operation can be omitted by the optimizer. This example shows again, how our technique can enable a parallel execution of complex user-defined operators. This is a significant progress compared to other approaches. Implementing the median as an aggregate function based on the usual iterator paradigm for UDAF is much more difficult as we have already pointed out in chapter 3.

6.3.4   A UDTO for a Complex Aggregation

In this subsection we will describe the application of a UDTO to implement a new feature for an existing document management system called ODS [18]. We first describe ODS and the profiling service as a new feature that must be implemented in ODS. Then we show how UDTO can be applied to enable the processing of all profiles in a single SQL statement (cf. [79] for an alternative implementation method that is applicable only by a DBMS vendor).

ODS provides a boolean retrieval model that answers queries on the existence of word patterns, words, phrases, and boolean expressions of them in documents. Syntax and semantics of the query language can be informally described as follows:

`<word>`	Exact match of `<word>`
`%`	Wild card character usable in a `<word>`, allowing to specify simple pattern matching
`.`	Distance operator, used to combine terms to phrases
`&`	Boolean AND of phrases
`|`	Boolean OR of phrases.

A *term* is defined as a word or a word pattern. Terms connected by distance operators form *phrases*. This simple language defines the basis of the retrieval service, as for example, the phrase "deduct% . database" asks for all documents in which there is an occurrence of a word starting with the string 'deduct' together with a word 'database' and having at most one other arbitrary word in between as indicated by the distance operator.

The document retrieval model of ODS is based on full-text indexing that, in the case of ODS, refers to plain relational tables, which are organized in such a way that document retrieval can be done efficiently. There are two important tables, a table `Words (Word, Word-ID)`, which maps each word which appears in at least one document to a numeric key `Word-ID`, and a table `Documents (Word-ID, Doc-ID, Pos)`, which maps word keys to numeric document keys `Doc-ID` and position numbers `Pos` depending on where the word appears in the documents; primary keys of the tables are underlined. A query that is specified as a boolean retrieval expression is mapped to an SQL query that uses the full-text index tables to search for all document keys that match the given expression. These queries can be quite complex. In practical applications, the full-text tables are more complex and optimized but these details are not of interest here.

We will now present our new application, the profiling service as described in [64]. Basically, a profile represents the user's reading interests and can be expressed as a single full-text retrieval query in ODS. The profiling service is the (batch) execution of a large set of profiles, which can be launched at fixed time intervals, for example once per night. A sample profile, also used in the following, may look like this:

```
('deduct% . database | multimedia database')
```

Please observe that profiles are usually evaluated in batch mode, which provides opportunities for multi-query optimization, i.e., to process a set of queries in an integrated, tightly coupled and optimized fashion. Obviously, it is a great advantage if one evaluates common subexpressions that occur in different profiles only once. Common subexpressions can be identified by searching for identical terms. This analysis can be done off-line and the result can be stored in three tables shown in Figure 34 for an example with two profiles. Each term that occurs in a profile, i.e., each word or word pattern, is assigned a term identifier (Term-ID) and stored in the Terms table. Terms connected by distance operators and boolean AND operators form *subprofiles*. In our example, there are 3 subprofiles. As the number of terms in a subprofile is variable, we have chosen to describe a subprofile in the Subprofiles table in the following way: for each term of a subprofile a corresponding tuple is inserted; the last column, ProfilePos, holds the position of the term within its subprofile; the Distance column expresses the number of words between the actual term and the next term in the subprofile as is defined by the distance operator used in that subprofile. The special value -1 of the Distance column expresses that this term is the last term of a phrase, and the special value -2 describes that this is the last term in the subprofile (the ProfilePos of this term gives the total number of terms in this subprofile). Finally, the Profiles table represents the profiles in disjunctive normal form over subprofiles. The tables store the description of the profiles and have to be updated if the set of profiles changes. Please note that common search terms occur only once in the Terms table. This reduces the costs of searching considerably.

Given these tables, how can we evaluate the profiles? Clearly, writing a single SQL query that does the complete work would be desirable. Unfortunately, finding the documents which match a subprofile is not possible in traditional SQL, i.e., without a UDTO. This is due to the fact that subprofiles define patterns consisting of a varying number of terms. In addition the terms have to occur in a certain order and within certain distances in a document. Even grouping with a UDAF in the HAVING clause cannot be used, because the UDAF would need to operate on several columns. To the best of our knowledge, this is currently not supported in commercial systems

Table Terms		Table Subprofiles				Table Profiles	
Term	*Term-ID*	*SubPro-ID*	*Term-ID*	*Distance*	*ProfilePos*	*Profile-ID*	*SubPro-ID*
architect%	6	1	1	1	1		
data%	4	1	2	-2	2	1	1
database	2	2	3	0	1	1	2
deduct%	1	2	2	-2	2	2	2
multimedia	3	3	4	-1	1	2	3
system	5	3	5	0	2		
		3	6	-2	3		

Figure 34. Profile Representation for Two Sample Profiles
(primary keys are underlined, common expressions are shaded):
Profile 1: 'deduct% . database | multimedia database'
Profile 2: 'multimedia database | data% & system architect%'.

([50], [53], [95]). On the other hand, a UDTO can provide the needed functionality. Let us call such a UDTO Match_SubProfile. This UDTO returns for each sub-profile all matching documents. The following query retrieves the Doc-ID of match-ing documents for all profiles using the full-text index tables Words and Documents and the UDTO Match_SubProfile:

```
SELECT DISTINCT Profile-ID, Doc-ID
FROM Profiles AS P,
     (SELECT SubPro-ID, Doc-ID
     FROM Match_SubProfile(
          SELECT SubPro-ID, Doc-ID, Pos, ProfilePos, Distance
          FROM   Terms, Subprofiles, Words, Documents
          WHERE  Words.Word LIKE Terms.Term AND
                 Words.Word-ID = Documents.Word-ID AND
                 Subprofile.Term-ID = Terms.Term-ID)
          ) AS S
WHERE P.SubPro-ID = S.SubPro-ID;
```

In this query the UDTO Match_SubProfile operates on a table expression (the corresponding input table is called Subprofile_Infos below) that contains for each subprofile the set of all positions in all documents that contain a word matching a term of a this subprofile. As a result of the application of the function Match_SubProfile, the table expression S returns a tuple containing a Subpro-ID and a Doc-ID for each document and subprofile pair, if the document matches the expression of the subprofile. Finally, in the outer query block all matches found are joined with the Profiles table. This results in a list of profiles and the matching Doc-IDs. The operator Match_SubProfile can be defined as follows:

```
CREATE TABLE_OPERATOR Match_SubProfile
(TABLE Subprofile_Infos (SubPro-ID INTEGER, Doc-ID INTEGER, Pos INTEGER,
 ProfilePos INTEGER, Distance INTEGER)
RETURNS
TABLE Subprofile_Docs (SubPro-ID INTEGER, Doc-ID INTEGER)
ALLOW PARALLEL (EQUAL (SubPro-ID, Doc-ID))
AS
{

// declaration of local variables
...


// for each subprofile and for each document:
// scan found term positions in order
FOR input_tuple AS
         SELECT SubPro-ID, Doc-ID, ProfilePos, Pos, Distance
         FROM Subprofile_Infos
         ORDER BY SubPro-ID, Doc-ID, ProfilePos, Pos
DO
// use the input tuples for a single document and subprofile
// to check whether all needed terms occur and
// whether they occur in the correct order and with correct distances
...


IF (/* document matches subprofile */) THEN
         // insert subprofile-ID and Document-ID into output table
         INSERT INTO Subprofile_Docs
         VALUES (input_tuple.SubPro-ID, input_tuple.Doc-ID);
END FOR;
}
```

For each subprofile and for each document the UDTO Match_SubProfile scans all tuples that describe the positions where terms of the subprofile occur in the document. These input tuples are then used to check whether all phrases of the subprofile occur in the document as specified in the definition of the subprofile. Because an efficient algorithm for this subprofile matching is rather complex (a special string matching algorithm is needed) and not relevant for our examination we have skipped it in the definition of Match_SubProfile. However, we want to remark that this subprofile matching can be done without additional SQL DML statements.

Please observe that all profiles are now evaluated with a single query that can be processed completely in parallel including the UDTO Match_SubProfile. To support this, we have specified the option ALLOW PARALLEL (EQUAL(SubPro-ID, Doc-ID)) for the UDTO. This is the most fine-grained data partitioning that is possible. The optimizer can choose any data partitioning that is compliant with this partitioning. A compliant partitioning can be obtained by the union of none, some, or all partitions. Hence, the optimizer could also choose the partitioning EQUAL(SubPro-ID) for the UDTO Match_SubProfile.

Without the possibility to use a UDTO, the profile evaluation must be done with embedded SQL. This results in much less parallelism as only a part of the profile evaluation can be processed by the following SQL query:

```
SELECT SubPro-ID, Doc-ID, Pos, ProfilePos, Distance
FROM Terms, Subprofiles, Words, Documents
WHERE    Words.Word LIKE Terms.Term AND
         Words.Word-ID = Documents.Word-ID AND
         Subprofile.Term-ID = Terms.Term-ID
ORDER BY SubPro-ID, Doc-ID, Pos
```

Such a traditional ESQL approach results in a poor response time because expensive parts of the evaluation have to be done in the application. Furthermore, this evaluation is only done in a sequential manner. In summary, the UDTO `Match_SubProfile` shows that the evaluation of application logic can be integrated into the database system.

6.3.5 Association Rule Mining

In this subsection we want to apply UDTO to the problem of association rule mining. We will first explain the problem and then we will show how UDTO can be applied to solve this problem. We present our ideas directly based on [97], where the integration of association rule mining with ORDBMS by means of UDF is presented. Especially, we do not propose any new algorithms here. The sole purpose is to show how UDTO allow to integrate algorithms for new applications into ORDBMS.

We begin with a brief introduction to the problem of association rule mining. The input for association rule mining consists of a single table with two columns of type integer: the first column contains a so-called Transaction-ID (TID) that identifies a specific business transaction like the buying of a set of products. The second column contains the identifiers of items (e.g. products) that are associated with a transaction. Each row contains exactly one TID and one item, i.e., the table is in first normal form.

The output of the association rule mining algorithm is a set of association rules. For two itemsets S and T the association rule S -> T has the intuitive meaning that transactions that contain the items in S tend to also contain the items in T. The set S is the *premise*, the set T the *consequence* of the rule. For example, this may mean that some set of products is often bought together with a set of other products. Each rule has two associated measures: *support* and *confidence*. The confidence of a rule expresses the percentage of those transactions containing the itemset S that also contain the itemset T. The support of a rule is the percentage of all transactions that contain both itemsets S and T. The problem of mining association rules is to find all rules that satisfy a user-specified minimum support and minimum confidence.

In practical applications, rules contain always only a small subset of the set of all items. Therefore the number of items per rule is limited in advance to a fixed number N of items. Hence, the resulting set of rules can be stored within a table where each row corresponds to one rule. The table has N columns to store items and a column that contains the actual number of items in this rule. This allows to represent rules with less than N items. Furthermore, another column contains the cardinality of the itemset in the premise of the rule, i.e. |S|. This allows to determine the items that appear in the premise of the rule, because these items are stored in the first attributes of a row. An additional column contains the support of this rule. An example for this rule table for N = 4 is Table 9.

Table 9. An Example Table with Association Rules for N = 4

item1	item2	item3	item4	num_items	len_premise	support
s1	s2	t1	NULL	3	2	0.10
s1	t1	NULL	NULL	2	1	0.07
...	...	...	...	...	...	...

The association rule mining problem can be decomposed into two subproblems:

1. Find all combinations of items, called *frequent itemsets*, whose support is greater than minimum support.

2. Use the frequent itemsets to generate the desired rules.

The second step is not crucial for overall performance [97]. Therefore we restrict our discussion mainly to the first step. However we remark that one can define a UDTO `Generate_Rules` that operates on a table that contains the frequent itemsets and delivers all rules that match the specifications with respect to support and confidence in the output table.

The first step, generating the frequent itemsets, can be done using the *Apriori algorithm* [1] which makes multiple passes over the data. In the kth pass it finds all itemsets having k items, called k-itemsets. Each pass consists of two phases. Let F_k represent the set of frequent k-itemsets, and C_k the set of candidate k-itemsets (potentially frequent k-itemsets). During the first phase, *candidate generation*, we generate C_k using F_{k-1}, the set of (k-1)-itemsets found in pass k-1. C_k is a superset of F_k. In the second phase, *support counting*, the frequent itemsets in C_k are determined. This is done as follows: for each transaction all itemsets in C_k are examined. If an itemset is contained in the transaction then its support count is incremented. At the end all itemsets with greater than minimum support are inserted into F_k. The algorithm terminates when either F_k or C_{k+1} becomes empty. The set of frequent 1-itemsets, F_1, serves as the starting point of the algorithm. It can be computed directly by means of the following SQL statement:

```
SELECT item, Count(*)
FROM Transactions
GROUP BY item
HAVING Count(*) >= msupport);
```

In this statement the table `Transactions` contains the set of transactions that form the input of the algorithm and `msupport` denotes the number of transactions in which an item must occur in order to fullfil the requirement with respect to the minimum support. F_1 is then used to generate the first needed set of candidate k-itemsets, i.e., C_2.

In the following we will create UDTO to support both phases, candidate generation and support counting. We want to remark that support counting is more expensive than candidate generation. Please note that all UDTO presented in the following are directly based on the algorithms or SQL commands given in [97].

Candidate Generation

First, we consider candidate generation. We define a class of UDTO Candidate_Gen_K for this task. Please note that we need a different UDTO for each pass, i.e., for each value of k between 2 and N. The reason is the lack of flexibility of UDTO with respect to different row types of the input tables. Attribute propagation cannot help in cases like this. With these UDTO, we can generate C_k in pass k as follows:

```
INSERT INTO C_K
SELECT * FROM Candidate_Gen_K (F_{k-1})
```

We assume here that C_k and F_k are tables to hold the candidate k-itemsets and the frequent k-itemsets, respectively. Please note that the table C_k must not be materialized before the support counting phase. With UDTO we can directly pipe C_k into the support counting phase and nevertheless yield compact code that is easy to understand.

We can create the UDTO Candidate_Gen_K as follows:

```
CREATE TABLE_OPERATOR Candidate_Gen_K
(TABLE F_{k-1} (item_1 INTEGER, item_2 INTEGER, ... , item_{k-1} INTEGER))
RETURNS
TABLE C_k (item_1 INTEGER, item_2 INTEGER, ... , item_k INTEGER)
AS
INSERT INTO C_k
SELECT I_1.item_1, I_1.item_2, ... , I_1.item_{k-1}, I_2.item_{k-1}
FROM F_{k-1} I_1, F_{k-1} I_2, ... , F_{k-1} I_k
WHERE      // first define a new k-itemset using the (k-1)-itemset of I_1
           // and the (k-1)th item of I_2, if this is smaller than
           // the (k-1)th item of I_1
           I_1.item_1 = I_2.item_1 AND
           I_1.item_2 = I_2.item_2 AND
           ...
           I_1.item_{k-2} = I_2.item_{k-2} AND
           I_1.item_{k-1} < I_2.item_{k-1}
AND
           // test whether all (k-1)-itemsets of new k-itemset
           // are frequent, i.e., are elements of F_{k-1}
           // use an equi-join with F_{k-1} to test this membership
           // do this for the k-2 (k-1)-itemsets obtained
           // by omitting one of the first k-2 items from I_1

           // omit I_1.item_1
           I_1.item_2 = I_3.item_1 AND
           I_1.item_3 = I_3.item_2 AND
           ...
           I_1.item_{k-1} = I_3.item_{k-2} AND
```

```
              I₂.item_{k-1} = I₃.item_{k-1}
AND

              // omit I₁.item₂
              I₁.item₁   = I₄.item₁   AND
              I₁.item₃   = I₄.item₂   AND
              ...
              I₁.item_{k-1} = I₄.item_{k-2} AND
              I₂.item_{k-1} = I₄.item_{k-1}
AND
...
AND

              // omit I₁.item_{k-2}
              I₁.item₁   = I_k.item₁   AND
              I₁.item₂   = I_k.item₂   AND
              ...
              I₁.item_{k-3} = I_k.item_{k-3} AND
              I₁.item_{k-1} = I_k.item_{k-2} AND
              I₂.item_{k-1} = I_k.item_{k-1}
```

The idea behind this algorithm is that all (k-1) subsets of frequent k-itemsets are frequent (k-1)-itemsets. Therefore we can generate C_k as follows: first, we join F_{k-1} with itself using an equi-join on the first (k-2) columns and a restriction with '<' on the (k-1)th column. This generates pairs of frequent (k-1)-itemsets that differ only in the (k-1)th item. We then add the (k-1)th item of one itemset to the other frequent (k-1)-itemset. Next, we have to test whether all k (k-1)-itemsubsets of this new k-itemset are elements of F_{k-1}. This test can be expressed through additional k-2 joins with F_{k-1} because we know already that the two (k-1)-itemsets that were used to construct the new k-itemset are frequent. Hence, only the k-2 other (k-1)-itemsubsets must be checked.

Clearly, it is a benefit if an operation of this complexity can be defined once and then be shared by all applications. We want to point out that the row type of the table which contains the input data set will probably always be the same. Otherwise (e.g. if the items are coded as strings instead of integers), it can be transformed by another UDTO into a table with the suitable row type. Therefore the UDTO Candidate_Gen_K can in principle be applied to all association rule mining problems.

Instead of defining different SQL macros for different values of K, we could define a single SQL macro Candidate_Gen that operates on an input table for N-itemsets. If K < N, the input table would contain NULL values for many items, similar to the table for the storage of the association rules (cf. Table 9). This would increase the table size. However, the most important drawback of such an approach is that the SQL statements in the body of the SQL macro must be formulated for the case K = N, which is very inefficient for the case K < N.

Since the algorithm for candidate generation is now encapsulated in the UDTO, we can exchange the implementation to improve performance without the need to rewrite all applications. For example, in [1] a special hash-tree in-memory data structure to store the input table F_{k-1} was proposed.

Support Counting

Support counting can be supported by UDTO as well. For the kth phase we define the UDTO `Support_Count_K`. [97] proposes six methods for support counting in ORDBMS. We consider here the three algorithms *GatherJoin*, *GatherCount* and *Vertical* that performed best for different cardinalities of C_k. Please note that this cardinality is known before the support counting begins if C_k is materialized. Hence, we can choose the best algorithm for support counting depending on the cardinality of C_k. This hybrid method was proposed in [97] as the best solution for an integration into an ORDBMS.

To provide an example, we will implement as a UDTO the algorithm *GatherJoin_K*, computing the frequent k-itemsets F_k for a given set of candidate k-itemsets C_k:

```
CREATE TABLE_OPERATOR Gather_Join_K
(TABLE Transactions (TID INTEGER, item INTEGER),
 TABLE Ck (item1 INTEGER, item2 INTEGER, ... , itemk INTEGER),
 msupport INTEGER)
RETURNS
TABLE Fk (item1 INTEGER, item2 INTEGER, ... , itemk INTEGER,
          count INTEGER)
AS
INSERT INTO Fk
SELECT Ck.item1, Ck.item2, ... , Ck.itemk, Count(*)
FROM Ck,
     Subsets_K (Transactions) AS S (item1, item2, ... ,itemk)
WHERE    Ck.item1 = S.item1 AND
         Ck.item2 = S.item2 AND
         ...
         Ck.itemk = S.itemk
GROUP BY Ck.item1, Ck.item2, ... , Ck.itemk
HAVING Count(*) > msupport
```

First, this UDTO generates the set of all k-itemsets for each transaction by invoking the UDTO `Subsets_K`, that we will describe below. Please note that one k-itemset can occur in many transactions, i.e., there are duplicates in the output table of `Subsets_K`. Then all subsets that do not occur in the candidate set C_k are removed (remember that C_k is a superset of F_k). This is achieved by an equi-join with C_k. Finally, the number of duplicates of each k-itemset is computed. It corresponds to the number of transactions in which the k-itemset occurs. If this number is greater than the required minimum support `msupport`, the k-itemset and its count are inserted into the output table F_k.

The UDTO `Subsets_K` can be implemented as a procedural UDTO, but we omit it here for the sake of brevity. This UDTO fetches for each transaction all rows with items from this transaction from the input table. Then for each transaction, all k-itemsets are generated and inserted into the output table. If the itemset of a transaction has a size smaller than k, no itemsets are generated for this transaction. An upper bound for the asymptotic complexity of the UDTO `Subsets_K` can be derived as follows: Let us assume that the number of rows in the input table is i, that the number of transactions is t, and that the largest itemset of a transaction has cardinality a. First, the input table must be sorted by the transaction ID. An upper bound for this is $O(i \cdot \log(i))$. Furthermore, there are at most $\binom{a}{k}$ k-itemsubsets for a transaction and at most $t \cdot \binom{a}{k} < t \cdot 2^a$ k-itemsubsets for all transactions. Consequently, an upper bound for the overall complexity is $O(i \cdot \log(i) + t \cdot 2^a)$.

Finally, we present an implementation of the UDTO Support_Count_K that chooses between the three algorithms for support counting at run-time using cost-estimates that can be computed using analytic formulas as given in [97]. Please note that all three algorithms *GatherJoin, GatherCount* and *Vertical* can be implemented as UDTO. Here is the definition of Support_Count_K:

```
CREATE TABLE_OPERATOR Support_Count_K
(TABLE Transactions (TID INTEGER, item INTEGER),
 TABLE C_k (item_1 INTEGER, item_2 INTEGER, ... , item_k INTEGER),
 minsupport INTEGER)
RETURNS
TABLE F_k (item_1 INTEGER, item_2 INTEGER, ... , item_k INTEGER,
           count INTEGER)
AS
{
FLOAT cost1, cost2, cost3;
INTEGER cardinality;

// estimate costs
SELECT Count(*) FROM C_k INTO cardinality;
set cost1 = GatherJoinCost(cardinality);
set cost2 = GatherCountCost(cardinality);
set cost3 = VerticalCost(cardinality);

// use estimated costs to choose algorithm
IF (cost1 < cost2 AND cost1 < cost3)
        INSERT INTO F_k
        SELECT * FROM Gather_Join_K(Transactions, C_k, minsupport)
ELSEIF (cost2 < cost1 AND cost2 < cost3))
        INSERT INTO F_k
        SELECT * FROM Gather_Count_K(Transactions, C_k, minsupport)
ELSE
        INSERT INTO F_k
        SELECT * FROM Vertical_K(Transactions, C_k, minsupport)
}
```

As for candidate generation we can exchange the implementation of the UDTO to improve the performance.

We can now define a procedural UDTO Association_Rules that does the complete association rule mining. Its input is the table with the transactions, the minimum confidence, and the minimum support and its output is the table with the rules. The following is a simple definition of this UDTO:

```
CREATE TABLE_OPERATOR Association_Rules
(TABLE Transactions (TID INTEGER, item INTEGER),
 minsupport FLOAT, minconfidence FLOAT)
RETURNS
TABLE Rules (item₁ INTEGER, item₂ INTEGER, ... , itemₙ INTEGER,
         number INTEGER, length INTEGER, support INTEGER)
AS
{
INTEGER i, k, card, msupport;

// compute number of transactions that correspond to the minimum support
SELECT Count(*) FROM Transactions GROUP BY TID INTO card;
SET msupport = Ceiling(card*minsupport);

// derive set of frequent 1-itemsets, F₁
CREATE TABLE F₁ (item₁ INTEGER, count INTEGER);
INSERT INTO F₁
 SELECT item, Count(*)
 FROM Transactions
 GROUP BY item
 HAVING Count(*) >= msupport);
SET k = 1;

// derive sets of frequent k-itemsets, Fₖ, for 2 <= k <= N
WHILE (card > 0 AND k < N)
  SET k = k + 1;
  ALTER TABLE Fₖ₋₁ ADD PRIMARY KEY (item₁, item₂, ... , itemₖ₋₁);
  CREATE TABLE Fₖ (item₁ INTEGER, ... ,itemₖ INTEGER, count INTEGER);
  INSERT INTO Fₖ
    SELECT * FROM
    Support_Count_K (Transactions, Candidate_Gen_K(Fₖ₋₁), msupport);
  SELECT Count(*) FROM Fₖ INTO card;
END WHILE;

// generate rules using the derived sets of frequent k-itemsets
INSERT INTO RULES
 SELECT *
 FROM Generate_Rules_K(
  (SELECT item₁,item₂,NULL, ... , NULL, count,2 FROM F2 UNION
   SELECT item₁,item₂,item₃, NULL, ... , NULL, count,3 FROM F3 UNION
   ...
   SELECT item₁,..., itemₖ₋₁, NULL,..., NULL, count, k-1 FROM Fₖ₋₁ UNION
   SELECT item₁, ... , itemₖ, NULL,..., NULL, count, k FROM Fₖ),
   minconfidence);

// clean up
FOR (i=1; i<=k; i++)
    DROP TABLE Fᵢ;
}
```

In the body of this UDTO, the UDTO `Candidate_Gen_K` for candidate generation is nested within the UDTO `Support_Count_K`. As an advantage of this nested invocation, we do not need to store the candidate k-itemsets explicitly in a table. Please note that the parameter k is incremented within the while loop. Since we have to invoke different UDTO depending on the value k, all SQL statements in the body of the UDTO `Association_Rules` must be generated at run-time, i.e., they have to be dynamic SQL. For the same reason the tables F_k are created at run-time. Moreover, the table names 'F_k' must be different for each instance of the UDTO to avoid name conflicts when several instances are executed at the same time. Of course, dynamic SQL is allowed within the body of procedural UDTO. We have simplified these aspects only to ease the presentation.

We want to point out that the most time-consuming parts of the presented association rule mining algorithm, candidate generation and support counting, can be executed in parallel. Moreover, this can be done completely automatically by the ORDBMS, since the UDTO `Gather_Join_K` and `Candidate_Gen_K` are SQL macros.

Finally, we demonstrate the flexibility that is introduced UDTO usage for association rule mining. Since the output of the rule mining process is a table, we can query the result immediately, as the following three queries show (in the examples the minimum support is always 2% and the minimum confidence is 30%):

1. Find all rules with more than ten items:

```
SELECT *
FROM    Association_Rules((Transactions),0.02,0.3) AS R
WHERE   R.length > 10
```

2. Find all rules in transactions that contain a certain item (denoted by `my_item`):

```
SELECT  *
FROM    Association_Rules((Transactions),0.02,0.3) AS R
WHERE   R.item₁ = my_item OR
        R.item₂ = my_item OR
        ...
        R.itemₙ = my_item
```

3. Find all rules and sort them by their support:

```
SELECT  *
FROM    Association_Rules((Transactions),0.02,0.3) AS R
ORDER   BY R.support
```

6.4 Related Work

While UDF have received much attention during the last years, extensibility at the level of database operators was not a focus of database research. An approach that offered extensibility by means of new database operators and that is superior in functionality to our approach is that of the EXODUS project [14]. In EXODUS new operators could be programmed with the E programming language. However, the EXODUS approach differs from our approach fundamentally, since the goal of EXODUS was not to provide extensibility for a complete, ready-to-run DBMS. Rather the goal was to enable the semi-automatic construction of an application-specific DBMS. Thus, EXODUS was a database software engineering project providing software tools for DBMS construction by vendors. By contrast, our approach allows to extend a complete ORDBMS by third parties like independent software vendors. We believe that our approach to program new operators with embedded SQL statements provides more support for parallel execution and fits well into current system architectures. In addition, developers can use a familiar technique to program UDTO. Hence, they are the ideal concept to support database extensions for class libraries by third parties as well as application-specific extensions. See [35] for a formal approach to specify database operations.

In [98] E-ADT are proposed as a new approach to the software architecture of ORDBMS. An ORDBMS is envisioned as a collection of E-ADT (enhanced ADT). These E-ADT encapsulate the complete functionality and implementation of ADT. We believe that this is an interesting approach that is in general more ambitious than UDTO. In contrast to the E-ADT approach, UDTO fit very well into the architectures of current commercial ORDBMS. Thus, UDTO leverage existing technology. Moreover, UDTO are designed to support parallel execution.

We have already mentioned that SQL macros can be viewed as a generalization of views [105]. The difference is that views can only refer to existing base tables and other views, but not to the results of subqueries or table expressions and that views cannot have parameters.

In chapter 3, we have proposed a framework for parallel processing of user-defined scalar and aggregate functions in ORDBMS. We introduced the concept of partitioning classes there to support the parallel execution of user-defined scalar and aggregate functions. In this chapter we have generalized this work to enable data parallelism for N-ary user-defined table operators. In chapter 5 we proposed the multi-operator method to allow the implementation of complex UDF like parallel join algorithms for UDPs. However, we view UDTO in the form of SQL macros as the more appropriate implementation technique. Moreover, procedural UDTO are a much more powerful concept than the multi-operator method.

6.5 Summary and Conclusions

In this chapter we have proposed UDTO as a novel approach to extensibility with regard to the execution engine and the query optimizer of ORDBMS. While current user-defined functions are used within the traditional database operators, our approach allows to develop new N-ary database operators. This technology provides a new dimension of extensibility with respect to query optimization and execution in ORDBMS.

We have presented the following core issues of UDTO:

- the possibility to define M input and N output tables for a user-defined routine
- the access to and the manipulation of these tables by means of SQL commands that are embedded into procedural code (procedural UDTO) or by means of a single SQL statement (SQL macro)
- attribute propagation to allow the application of UDTO to a broad range of input tables based on a generalization relationship between row types
- a method to specify parallel execution schemes for UDTO and the general algorithm for their parallel processing
- the explicit application of UDTO within SQL and their use as high performance implementations for operations involving UDF.

The discussion of applications has clearly demonstrated that UDTO have the following advantages:

- Interoperability:
  Input and output of UDTO are tables. Therefore we can combine UDTO with each other and integrate them into queries.
- Usage flexibility:
  UDTO can be used flexibly in ad-hoc queries.
- Information hiding:
  Algorithms and data structures can be hidden from the user and exchanged, if necessary.
- Centralized definition and maintenance of functional extensions:
  A UDTO is defined once and can then be generally used. This is a tremendous benefit from a software engineering point of view.
- Enhanced readability and understandability of complex SQL statements
  Hiding of complex operations can reduce the length and textual complexity of SQL statements considerably. This support for hierarchical design has been successful in many areas.
- Parallelization:
  UDTO provide an excellent support for parallelization. They can either be parallelized automatically or the developer can specify data partitioning schemes explicitly.
- Implementation flexibility:
  Developers can use DBMS capabilities like indexing, query processing, and space management whenever this is appropriate. On the other hand, they can implement specific, sophisticated algorithms and data structures (hash tables, etc.) whenever this is beneficial.
- Run-time optimization:
  UDTO allow to make flexible use of different implementation methods at run time. The corresponding control flow can be implemented in procedural UDTO.

This was demonstrated for association rule mining in subsection 6.3.5. Please note that run-time optimization is especially of interest for complex applications which require computationally expensive operations on very large data sets.

We believe that the possibility to define new operators is very promising, especially since the SQL-based implementation technique is in our view elegant and easy to understand for developers. In addition, sophisticated optimization technology can be used to produce high-quality plans that are automatically fine tuned to the estimated data volumes.

With regard to SQL macros the UDTO approach is similar to pushing views into the middle of SQL statements. SQL macros allow to push code into a new operator, where it is defined once (e.g. in a DBMS class library) and where it is available for general use in SQL. Hence, only a single definition has to be maintained. This eases the task of the application programmer, makes it less error-prone, improves the declarative character of SQL DML commands and enhances the readability. Moreover, SQL macros can always be completely integrated into the query execution plans of SQL statements by macro expansion. As a consequence, the usual parallelization techniques can be used.

The concept of procedural UDTO is much more powerful, because one can execute queries on the input tables and in addition one can use a procedural language like SQL PSM to implement complex algorithms. This is especially of interest in combination with an API that is provided for the development of DBMS class libraries by some ORDBMS ([50], [53], [54]). UDTO offer the possibility to implement new algorithms like join algorithms, for example. Moreover, our approach supports data parallelism for these new database operators. Besides being able to define parallel processing schemes by specifying allowed partitioning functions, the possibility to use SQL goes a long way towards enabling as much parallelism as possible, since all embedded SQL statements can be processed automatically in parallel. An additional advantage of our SQL-based approach to the implementation of UDTO is that query optimization can be fully exploited.

UDTO extend the extensibility of current commercial PORDBMS significantly. However, they offer less flexibility with regard to the implementation of new database operators than database software engineering frameworks like EXODUS. The reason is that EXODUS supports the implementation of new operators that could handle *arbitrary* row types. On the other hand, UDTO are always limited to a subclass of rowtypes. One could try to extend the UDTO concept to generic input and output tables that are dynamically described. However, in case of efficient implementations for UDF and in case of operations on application-specific schemata the flexibility of UDTO is already sufficient. The reason is that there are in both cases specific row types for the input tables because UDF have a fixed signature. Therefore a lot of practical problems can be solved by this technology.

While the limitation of UDTO to a subclass of rowtypes is sometimes not acceptable, it is also an immense benefit: It makes the implementation of new database operators much easier because there is no need to handle arbitrary row types. This allows the use of SQL to access input and output tables. As a result the programming is much more easy and large parts of existing technology can be leveraged.

A prototypical implementation of the UDTO concept in a PORDBMS has been accomplished and we will report on this effort in the next chapter.

CHAPTER 7

Implementation of UDTO

7.1 Introduction

In this chapter we present the concept of an implementation of SQL macros and procedural UDTO in ORDBMS. We do this based on the prototypical implementation in the PORDBMS prototype MIDAS which is under development at the Technische Universität Müchen and the University of Stuttgart. While we focus on the discussion of the actual implementation within MIDAS, we also propose possible optimizations of this implementation.

We introduce MIDAS in section 7.2. Then we discuss the implementation of SQL macros (section 7.3) and procedural UDTO (section 7.4). Section 7.5 presents some further query optimization issues for UDTO. While we initially consider only the explicit invocation of UDTO, in section 7.6, we outline the generation of alternative execution plans for UDF during query optimization. Section 7.7 evaluates our implementation.

7.2 The MIDAS Prototype

In this section we introduce the PORDBMS prototype MIDAS. MIDAS is based on the source code of the sequential RDBMS TransBase [109] which is the commercial version of the DBMS Merkur [25] - a research prototype developed at the Technische Universität Müchen during the 80s. MIDAS has been developed within the long-term research project SFB 314, project B2, which started in 1990 [100] and is funded by the German National Science Foundation (DFG). One of the early goals of the project was the construction of a prototypical parallel scalable RDBMS. Recently extensibility was added as a line of research.

In the following we restrict ourselves to a high-level description of MIDAS. We present only some details that are needed to provide the necessary background information. Additional details follow later, when we describe the implementation of UDTO. More information on the MIDAS prototype is contained for example in ([7], [9], [18], [78], [79], [80], [113]).

M. Jaedicke: Parallel Object-Relational Query Processing, LNCS 2169, pp. 106-144, 2001.
© Springer-Verlag Berlin Heidelberg 2001

7.2.1   Architectural Overview

Figure 35 shows the architecture of the MIDAS prototype. MIDAS was developed as a shared-disk database system. However, MIDAS was not built on top of special shared-disk hardware, but rather relies on NFS as a software solution for data sharing. MIDAS can either run on a shared-memory computer (or SMP for symmetric multi-processing) or on a farm of workstations and servers (which can be SMPs themselves) with locally attached hard disks. In the latter case, several computers communicate via a high-speed interconnection (like switched fast ethernet or gigabit ethernet). The communication in MIDAS is based on the message passing library Parallel Virtual Machines (PVM) [27].

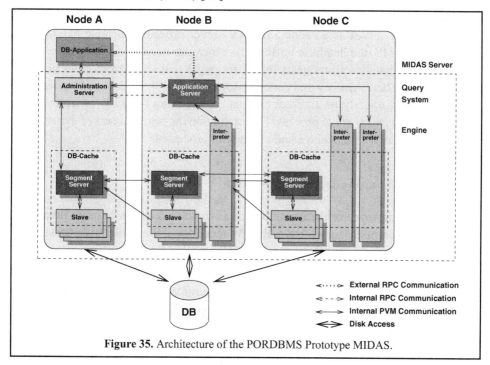

Figure 35. Architecture of the PORDBMS Prototype MIDAS.

MIDAS has a client/server architecture (cf. Figure 35). A database application (client) connects to the MIDAS server via the *administration server*. There is only one administration server process for a MIDAS DBMS instance. It is started when a database is booted by the database administrator. The administration server assigns each client exclusively to one *application server*. If there is no available application server process for a new client, then the administration server creates one. The client sends all his requests directly to the corresponding application server. Applications can use either embedded SQL or the proprietary call-level interface of MIDAS (called TBX for TransBase eXecute) to execute database commands. The main components of the application server are the SQL compiler, the scheduler and the catalog manager that manages the system tables. DDL statements are directly processed by the application server. DML commands are translated into query execution plans (QEPs).

In MIDAS, a QEP is an operator tree. The QEP is sent by the scheduler to one or more *interpreter* processes. An interpreter executes (a subtree of) a given QEP. This includes the evaluation of all operators in a QEP. Every interpreter has full access to the database buffer (called DB-Cache in Figure 35) and can also perform I/O operations. This inclusion of buffer and storage management functionality has been done due to performance reasons [8]. The main reason is that PVM is not thread-safe and hence MIDAS cannot use threads to lower the inter-process communication costs. Each computer (node) of the MIDAS server system has exactly one *segment server* process (cf. Figure 35). The segment server does the lock, buffer and storage management, i.e., it serves as a cache and lock server process. Because MIDAS is a shared-disk DBMS, the database buffer offers location-transparent page access. The segment server handles all requests for buffer pages that come from other nodes. It takes care of cache coherency and concurrency control [65]. All requests that involve time-consuming operations and that can lead to blocking (like I/O operations) are delegated to a *segment slave* process. For each node the segment server dynamically manages a pool of segment slave and interpreter processes.

7.2.2   Query Compilation and Execution

In this subsection we describe query compilation and execution in more detail. We start with the compiler. As we have already mentioned, the application server contains the SQL compiler and manages the system tables.

DML statements are internally represented as *operator trees*. There are *item operators* and *bulk operators*. Bulk operators are operators that represent set-oriented operations like the restriction, projection, union, and Cartesian product operations of the relational algebra. Please note that these bulk operators are physical operators in MIDAS, i.e., they perform a specific algorithm like a nested-loops join, a hash join or a sort-merge join. Item operators implement operations on scalar values like arithmetic or boolean operations. The item operators can be combined to a tree that serves as argument of some bulk operator. For example, a restriction operator has an item operator tree as argument that describes the restriction predicate. An operator tree is internally represented as a C-structure. However, it is possible to transform operator trees in a text format called *gentree* (cf. subsection 5.4.2). Such a gentree can also be used as an input for the compiler via a special interface. It is also possible for an application to directly execute a gentree via the TBX-interface.

Figure 36 shows the components of the application server. All commands are first processed by the *scanner* and the *parser*. DDL statements are parsed and then executed directly by the application server. This is reasonable, since DDL commands

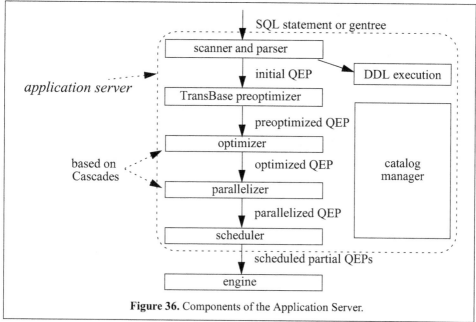

Figure 36. Components of the Application Server.

modify the system tables and the catalog manager is a component of the application server. For DML statements the parser works in two passes. In the first pass, the syntactic and semantic correctness of the statement is checked and an operator tree is built. During the second pass, additional semantic checks are performed and the schema of the intermediate results that are produced by the operators is computed. The result is an initial QEP. However, this QEP is by no means optimized. It is a direct translation of the SQL statement into an operator tree.

This initial QEP is then preoptimized using some passes of the *TransBase optimizer*. This optimizer applies heuristic transformations in several passes to an operator tree. While this component did the complete optimization in TransBase, it is now largely replaced by a new optimizer called Model_M (M for MIDAS) ([5], [48], [62]). Some passes of the TransBase optimizer are still used as a kind of preoptimization step for Model_M. These passes transform the operator tree into a normalized format, they transform IN and EXISTS subqueries into joins, and push down restrictions and projections as far as possible, for example.

The new *query optimizer* Model_M is still under construction. It is based on the Cascades Optimizer Framework, which has been originally developed by Goetz Graefe at the Oregon Graduate Institute [30]. This work is now continued by Len Shapiro and his group at the Portland State University [5]. Cascades supports rule- and cost-based query optimization. The core of Cascades is the search engine which applies rules to transform a given QEP and manages the set of generated variants of the QEP. For each variant, it computes estimated execution costs based on database statistics and the cost model of the MIDAS engine. When the search is completed, the plan with the lowest costs is selected.

The *parallelizer*, called TOPAZ uses Cascades as a search engine, too ([26], [80]). Parallelization is done in multiple phases to reduce the search space. The different phases support different kinds of parallelism, like inter-operator parallelism, intra-operator parallelism, and pipelining. An important goal of the parallelization is to keep the overhead for parallel execution low. This overhead results from costs for communication, data distribution and a higher number of involved processes. The output of the parallelization is a parallel QEP. Parallelism is expressed by means of *send and receive operators* that transfer data streams between producer and consumer processes.

The parallel QEP has certain cost annotations that are used by the *scheduler* [91]. The scheduler has the task to balance the load in the system. For this purpose the segment servers exchange information about the current load of the nodes in the system. The scheduler uses this information about the system state and the cost annotations of the QEP to assign the different parts of the parallel QEP to the nodes in such a way that the load is evenly distributed among the different nodes.

The compilation of gentrees differs somewhat. There is a special first pass of the parser that converts the gentree to the internal representation of the operator tree. The second pass is the same as for DML statements. Typically, a gentree is then executed directly by the scheduler without prior optimization and parallelization. However, it is possible to invoke these phases manually for gentrees.

As we have mentioned above, the engine of MIDAS consists of segment servers, segment slaves and interpreters. We add some details on the functioning of the interpreters in the following. Each interpreter evaluates an operator (sub-)tree. This evaluation follows the traditional open-next-close approach. The dataflow within an interpreter is control-driven, i.e. top-down and one-tuple-at-a-time.

As we have already described, send and receive operators transfer intermediate results between different interpreters to realize data parallelism and pipelining. The send operator acts as writer, the receive operator as reader for a *communication segment* which is a special implementation of temporary tables [10]. In contrast to the dataflow within an interpreter, the dataflow between interpreters via communication segments is data-driven, i.e. bottom-up, and pages are used as the unit of transfer. Communication segments have many parameters that serve to optimize flow control and storage management for a given pair of send/receive operators. There exist also named communication segments that allow the transfer of an intermediate result between different statements. They can be viewed as an implementation of named temporary tables that are valid during a single transaction.

7.2.3   The MIDAS System Tables

In this subsection we briefly introduce the reader to the system tables of MIDAS and their management. Users can read the system tables by usual SELECT statements. However, there is a special internal interface to the catalog manager that allows retrieval and modification of the system tables by other components of the application server, like the parser, optimizer and the executor for DDL statements. This is necessary because the system tables cannot be treated as user-defined base tables. For efficiency reasons, the results of queries to the system tables are cached in special data structures. This allows to avoid the repeated evaluation of such queries. When the system tables are updated, information in the cache must be invalidated. Of course, another reason for the special treatment of the system tables is that the information from the system tables is needed during query compilation.

The TransBase system tables have been adopted unchanged to MIDAS and contain information on tables, views, and columns, the dependencies for views, users and their authorizations, and the defined indexes [109]. Some system tables were added to MIDAS that store database statistics and metadata for user-defined functions [90]. In the following we describe those parts of the system tables to which we refer later on.

The table systable stores the following information about all persistent tables or views: the name of the table, the number of its columns, the type of the table (view, system table or base table), the creator of the table, the date of the creation and the segment number of the table. The segment number is a unique integer value. Positive values are used for system and base tables to identify the file in which the table is stored. Views have a negative segment number.

The table syscolumn contains rows for each defined column with the following fields: the column name, the segment number of the corresponding table, the data type of the column, and the position of the column in the table. Other fields contain information on constraints that are defined on this column.

Metadata on views is stored in the table sysview. The columns contain the segment number of the view, the text of the CREATE VIEW statement as string, information on the updatability of the view and the viewtree. The latter is the operator tree of the SELECT statement that defines the view. This operator tree is stored as a gentree, i.e. as a string.

Several system tables have been added in [90]. Some of these tables contain statistics on the data in the base tables. These statistics are generated by a utility (cf. [91]) that must be executed by the database administrator. There are coarse-grained statistics on the tables and indexes (like cardinality and number of occupied pages) and fine-grained statistics on the value distributions within the columns (like equi-depth histograms).

Other tables contain metadata on UDTs and UDSF. These two concepts have been recently implemented in MIDAS (cf. [39], subsection 7.2.4). The table `sysdatatypes` stores information about the built-in data types and the defined UDTs. The table `sysfunctions` contains a row for each defined UDSF. It stores the function name, an internal identifier, the data type of the return value and the number of parameters. Further parameters describe properties of the function that have been discussed in section 2.2. For example, whether the function uses a scratchpad, whether it is deterministic, whether it has side-effects, etc. Moreover, the implementation of the function is described. The type of the function (sourced function or external function) is stored. For external functions the name of the DLL that contains the executable code and the entry point for this DLL are stored.

The table `sysfuncparams` stores one row for each parameter of a function and one row for its return value. Each row contains the name of the function, the type of the row (parameter or return value description), the position of the parameter in the signature of the function and the description of the data type.

The table `sysfuncstat` contains the parameters that are used for the estimation of the execution costs of a UDSF. These parameters are for example the average number of I/O operations and CPU instructions for each invocation of the function (cf. subsection 2.2.1). Finally, information about the allowed partitioning strategies for parallel execution of a UDSF (cf. subsection 3.3.4) is stored in the table `sysfuncimp`. In the next section we will describe how the metadata for UDTO is stored, but first we describe the implementation of UDSF in MIDAS.

7.2.4   UDSF in MIDAS

Currently, UDSF can be used in SQL statements at all places where expressions are allowed. However, DDL statements to create and drop UDSF have not yet been implemented, i.e., one has to update the system tables manually to register a function. A new item operator, called `func`, has been implemented that represents a UDSF in a QEP. This node contains the path and the name of the DLL that contains the executable code and the corresponding entry point. There is only a single copy of the DLL in the file system that can be accessed from all nodes via NFS.

The `func` operator is evaluated once for each invocation of the UDSF within an SQL statement. During the first execution of the `func` operator for a given UDSF, the dynamic linker is invoked to bind the DLL dynamically to the interpreter process, if this is necessary. Another call translates the symbolic entry point to the DLL into the main memory address of the executable function. Because the scheduler does not assign the `func` operator for a given UDSF always to the same interpreter process, it can be necessary to load and link the DLL multiple times. However, this occurs only once per node, since the DLL is a shared object that is used by all interpreters on a node. Since a DLL typically contains many UDSF - for example all functions in a package - dynamic linking only occurs rarely in a running system and the overhead is negligible. Because it is sometimes a problem to use an existing library due to name conflicts we also added the possibility to link libraries statically to interpreter processes. However, this feature is only available for the developers of the MIDAS prototype and hence can be used only for internal purposes.

The sons of the `func` operator contain the arguments of the UDSF. Since UDSF have different signatures, the number of sons is variable, which is not the case for almost all other operators. Since the data types of the arguments are also variable, a generic interface is needed that can be used to call all UDSF in the same way, i.e., independent of their signature. This interface is similar to the interface to the `main()` routine of C programs: The function is called with 3 arguments. The first argument is a pointer to the result value, the second argument contains the number of the arguments of the UDSF and the third argument contains a pointer to an array with the argument values. All argument values and the return value are internally casted to a common data type. This data type is defined as the union type of all built-in data types. The internal return value of the function call is always an integer value that indicates if the function call was successful or not. In the latter case it contains an error code. All external UDSF must use this interface to handle their parameters.

7.3 Implementation of SQL Macros

Now, we are ready to describe the implementation of UDTO in MIDAS. We start with SQL macros in this section, because their implementation is less complex than that of procedural UDTO. In the first subsection we show how SQL macros are defined and registered and discuss the corresponding entries in the system tables. In subsection 7.3.2 we explain how SQL macros can be used in DML statements and how the macro expansion has been implemented. The last subsection, 7.3.3, presents a concept for the implementation of SQL macros in middleware. This implementation is based on automatic rewriting of SQL statements into other SQL statements, i.e., it works on a textual query representation.

7.3.1 DDL Statements

As we have described in subsection 6.2.2, UDTO are created by means of the statement CREATE TABLE_OPERATOR (or CREATE UDTO for short, cf. Figure 28 and Figure 29 for the syntax). As we will explain in the following the signature of the SQL macro and its body (the INSERT statement) are stored in the system tables. The way in which the system tables are used may not always be very clean, but typically users access only views on the system tables. These views usually hide information that is only of interest for internal purposes and provide a conceptually clean view on the metadata.

For our discussion we use the following statement that creates the UDTO `my_macro` as an example:

```
CREATE UDTO my_macro
(TABLE my_input (my_id INTEGER, my_text CHAR(*)), my_string CHAR(*) )
RETURNS TABLE my_output (my_id INTEGER, my_text CHAR(*), my_input.+)
AS
INSERT INTO my_output
SELECT a.my_id, a.my_text, a.+
FROM my_input a
WHERE a.text LIKE my_string
```

This SQL macro selects all rows of the input table, whose attribute `my_text` matches the scalar parameter `my_string` of the SQL macro. The keyword AS separates the signature of the SQL macro from its body, the INSERT statement.

The signature of the SQL macro is processed as follows: a row in the table `sysfunctions` stores its name (`my_macro`), the number of its parameters (3), and its type (SQL macro). Other types are UDSF or procedural UDTO. The parameters are seen as the sequence of the columns of the input tables and the scalar parameters. Hence, we have three parameters for the SQL macro `my_macro`: `my_id`, `my_text`, and `my_char`. For each parameter a description is stored in the table `sysfuncparams`. This table contains also a description of each column of the output table (`my_id`, `my_text` and, `my_input.+`). Columns of the output table that represent additional input columns of a table (like `my_input.+`), are stored with the name of the input table (`my_input`) as column name and a special data type (for the '+'). Moreover, metadata for input and output tables (`my_input` and `my_output`), is always stored in the tables `systable` and `syscolumn`. The entries are similar to those for base tables. However, like views all input and output tables get negative segment numbers to distinguish them from base tables. Creating these entries has the benefit that the parsing of the INSERT statement in the body of the SQL macro referring to these tables is easier to implement, because the system tables can be used in the same way as for base tables or views. Finally, for each input or output table an entry in a new system table `sysfuncimp` stores to which SQL macro this table belongs.

After all information about the signature is stored, the body of the SQL macro is processed. The INSERT statement is parsed and translated into an operator tree. Then an entry for the output table is created in the table sysview. Similar to the metadata for a view, this entry is used to store the text of the INSERT statement and its operator tree as a gentree. The parser for the INSERT statement had to be extended slightly to handle references to additional columns of input tables and to the scalar parameters of the SQL macro in a correct way.

The following statement DROP UDTO deletes all entries in the system tables for the UDTO `my_macro`:

```
DROP UDTO my_macro
```

7.3.2   SQL Macro Expansion in DML Statements

Once an SQL macro is defined it can be used in DML statements. However the usage in MIDAS is currently limited to the use within the FROM clause of queries. The following semantically equivalent queries show how the SQL macro my_macro defined in the last subsection can be used. The queries select information about all tables whose name begins with 'sys' from the system table systable:

```
SELECT * FROM my_macro (systable (segno, tname), 'sys%') a (id, name)

SELECT * FROM my_macro ( (SELECT segno, tname FROM systable), 'sys%') a (id,
name)
```

As these examples show, one can either use a base table with a binding for the columns or a table expression as an argument for the SQL macro. In the current implementation one must define a correlation name (a) and column names (id, name) for the output table of the SQL macro. One could also take the names that are used in the definition of the UDTO as default names of output columns (for additional input columns which appear in the output table one can use the column name of the input tables, unless there is a name conflict).

The macro expansion is done in the first pass of the parser. If the name of an SQL macro is parsed in the FROM clause then the signature of this SQL macro is retrieved from the system tables. This metadata is used to check the syntactic and semantic correctness of the UDTO invocation. For example, it is checked whether the arguments are tables and scalar values as defined in the signature and whether the schemata of the input tables are correct. For all arguments of the SQL macro, a routine of the parser is invoked transforming the argument to an operator tree. If a base table with a column binding is used as argument an operator tree for the access to this table is created and the columns are permuted according to the binding. This assures that the first columns of the resulting table of the operator tree match the columns of the corresponding input table in the UDTO definition. However this permutation is not really done during the execution, because a special pass of the TransBase optimizer eliminates unnecessary projections. For scalar arguments an operator delivering a constant value is generated (correlated references to attribute values are currently not allowed as scalar arguments).

After the operator trees for the arguments (called argument trees) have been created, the gentree of the INSERT statement of the body of the SQL macro is retrieved from the table sysview. This gentree is then converted into an operator tree that we call macro tree. This macro tree is then integrated into the tree of the active DML statement as follows: the top operator of the macro tree is removed. This top operator inserts rows into the target table. The remainder of the tree produces the rows to be inserted. In this subtree all references to the input tables are replaced by the appropriate argument trees. Because there can be multiple references to an input table in the body of an SQL macro, multiple copies of an argument tree can occur in the result tree. The result tree represents the output table of the UDTO and is returned to the parser. The parser handles this tree in the same way as the trees that represent the access to another base table or view in the FROM clause, respectively.

However, there is an additional difficulty during the merge step. The macro tree is the direct translation of the INSERT statement. Hence, if additional attributes of an input table must be considered, the schema descriptions of the result tables of the plan operators have to be adjusted to this situation. Especially, one must take care of references to attributes (that internally refer to attribute positions and not to attribute names) and projection operations. This is done by the modification of projection operations and the insertion of additional projection operations permuting additional attributes to the end of the row. Thus, attribute references to the first attributes that occur in the formal input tables of the SQL macro can remain unchanged in the macro tree. Later the TransBase optimizer eliminates all projection operations not needed and modifies the attribute references accordingly.

Recursion is not allowed for SQL macros, i.e., one cannot refer in the body of an SQL macro to the SQL macro itself. However, it is possible to refer to other SQL macros or procedural UDTO. Other SQL macros are immediately expanded during the parsing of the INSERT statement in the body of a UDTO. Procedural UDTO are integrated into the operator tree of an SQL macro as usual. In both cases the resulting gentree is stored in the system table sysview. One can also nest UDTO, i.e., one can use the output table of a UDTO directly as the input table for the same or another UDTO. This case can be handled as usual, too: the operator tree for the output table of the inner UDTO is constructed and serves as an argument tree (input table) for the outer UDTO.

7.3.3   Expanding SQL Macros in Preprocessors and Middleware

SQL macros have the additional benefit to enable the use of query rewriting techniques at the textual level of SQL statements to expand them. Hence, a preprocessor can be applied to expand SQL macros in SQL statements. This might be an implementation alternative, if the SQL compiler of the DBMS cannot be extended. Such a technique could also be useful in middleware products like IBM's Data Joiner that allow to query several different (O)RDBMS with a single SQL query. Parts of such a query are pushed down to the DBMS where the data is stored to enable local processing, if this reduces the evaluation costs. If the local DBMS does not support an SQL macro then the macro can be expanded in the middleware layer and all or parts of it can be pushed down. In the following, we show that this macro expansion is always possible. However, it might not always lead to more efficient query execution plans. Hence, the query optimizer in the middleware must be able to estimate the execution costs in a local DBMS. Modern middleware optimizers have this capability [38].

An SQL macro consists of an INSERT statement with a subquery Q (SQL macros inserting a constant table into the output table can be viewed as UDTF, because their output does not depend on the input). We denote the comprising command containing the SQL macro by C. First, we will assume that the command C is a SELECT statement. Later we generalize the rewriting technique to INSERT, UPDATE, and DELETE.

Please note that the rewriting is trivial for SQL macros explicitly applied. The reason is that these SQL macros are invoked explicitly with tables or table expressions as arguments. Thus, they can be merged directly into C by replacing references to the formal parameter tables and scalar parameters in Q by references to the actual arguments. In addition, the '+' notation has to be replaced by the additional attributes. Then the SQL macro can be replaced by the table expression Q. Hence, in the following we deal only with SQL macros that are used by the optimizer to implement a UDF efficiently.

There are four possible usages of UDF that can be implemented by means of SQL macros (cf. subsection 6.2.3): A UDSF can be used to compute a value in an expression (projection), a UDAF can be used in an expression in the PROJECT and HAVING clause (aggregation), and a UDP can be used as a predicate in a restriction or in a join. We will now describe transformations (rewrite rules) for each of these cases that allow to expand the SQL macro.

Expanding SQL Macros that Serve as Projection

First, we consider the use of an SQL macro to compute a UDSF in a projection operation. For such an SQL macro, the output table has the same number of rows as the input table, but an additional column that represents the value that is computed by the UDSF. Hence, Q must have the following syntax:

```
SELECT ME1, input.*
FROM input, MF1
WHERE MW1
GROUP BY MG1(input.*)
HAVING MH1
```

Here ME1 (the 'M' refers to *macro*) denotes the expression that computes the return value of the UDSF, input.* denotes *all* columns of the table input, MF1 denotes the remainder of the FROM clause, MW1 denotes the predicate of the WHERE clause, MG1 denotes the grouping columns, and MH1 denotes the predicate of the HAVING clause. Please note that Q might consist of several SELECT blocks of this kind that are linked by set operations (UNION, EXCEPT, INTERSECT). We have simplified this aspect to ease the presentation. It is straightforward to extend this algorithm to SQL macros with set operations at the outermost level of Q. If the SQL macro contains a GROUP BY clause at the top level, *all* columns of the input table (including additional columns) must be used as grouping attributes. This is indicated by the expression MG1(input.*). Otherwise the SQL macro is not an implementation of a projection as not all columns of the input table are preserved in the output.

The statement C can use a UDSF either in the SELECT or in the WHERE clause. In the latter case, C looks as follows:

```
SELECT S1
FROM F1
WHERE W1(U(E₁, E₂, ..., Eₙ))
GROUP BY G1
HAVING H1
```

The variables S1, F1, W1, G1, and H1 represent the text of the corresponding clause. Moreover, the expression $W1(U(E_1, E_2, \ldots, E_N))$ indicates that the UDSF U is evaluated in the WHERE clause with the expressions $E_1, E_2, \ldots, E_N$ as arguments. Obviously, we can transform C into the following equivalent statement:

```
SELECT S1'
FROM (SELECT U(E₁, E₂, ..., Eₙ) AS RESULT, F1.* FROM F1) AS F
WHERE W1' (F.RESULT)
GROUP BY G1'
HAVING H1'
```

In this statement the UDSF U is first evaluated in the table expression F in which it occurs in the SELECT clause and the return value is stored in a column RESULT. The attribute references in S1, W1, G1, and H1 have to be updated to the new column names of F and the reference to the UDSF U must be replaced by the reference to the column RESULT. Because the UDSF does now occur in the SELECT clause, we need to solve the macro expansion only for this case. We emphasize that these rewrite transformations themselves are *not* done for efficiency reasons. They only serve to enable the macro expansion. In contrast, it is the task of the query optimizer (of the middleware or of the (local) DBMS) to find the cheapest plan.

A statement C that uses the UDSF U in the SELECT clause, in general looks as follows:

```
SELECT S1(U(E₁, E₂, ..., Eₙ))
FROM F1
WHERE W1
GROUP BY G1
HAVING H1
```

Now we will expand the SQL macro that implements the UDSF U in a projection operation. This can be eased by a first step that is similar to the last transformation for UDSF in WHERE clauses:

```
SELECT S1'(RESULT)
FROM (SELECT U(E₁, E₂, ..., Eₙ) AS RESULT, F1.* FROM F1) AS F
WHERE W1'
GROUP BY G1'
HAVING H1'
```

Now the UDSF occurs in a table expression that has only the tasks to compute the UDSF U and to append the result as a new column to the output table). This is exactly the purpose of the SQL macro for U. Hence, we can rewrite the table expression:

```
SELECT U(E₁, E₂, ..., Eₙ) AS RESULT, F1.* FROM F1
```

into:

```
SELECT ME1'(E₁, E₂, ..., Eₙ), F1.*
FROM F1, MF1'
WHERE MW1'
GROUP BY MG1'(F1.*)
HAVING MH1'
```

This table expression is generated from Q as follows: the references to the input table are replaced by references to F1 and ME1, MF1, MW1, MG1, MH1 are modified by replacing references to columns of the input table and to scalar parameters by the expressions E_1, E_2, ..., E_N. We indicate this kind of modifications by a ' ' '. In summary, we have shown that we can replace a reference to a UDSF in a SELECT or WHERE clause by the expanded SQL macro.

Expanding SQL Macros that Serve as Aggregation

Second, we consider the case that an SQL macro is used to implement a UDAF more efficiently. In this case the SQL macro produces only a single scalar value - namely the aggregate. Hence, the SQL macro must have the following general form (as in the first case, we do not consider set operations):

```
SELECT ME1
FROM input, MF1
WHERE MW1
```

A UDAF, denoted by A, can occur either in the SELECT or the HAVING clause of C. In the latter case, the general form of C is:

```
SELECT S1
FROM F1
WHERE W1
GROUP BY G1(GA)
HAVING H1 (A(E₁, E₂, ..., Eₙ), A₁, ..., Aₖ)
```

The grouping attributes are denoted by GA (which might be an empty set of attributes) and A_1, ..., A_K denotes all other aggregate functions that occur in the HAVING clause. We can transform such a statement C into the following statement where the UDAF A occurs in the SELECT clause:

```
SELECT F.S
FROM (    SELECT S1 AS S,GA, A(E₁, E₂, ..., Eₙ) AS AGGR, A₁, ..., Aₖ
               FROM F1
```

```
            WHERE W1
            GROUP BY G1(GA) ) AS F
WHERE H1'(F.AGGR, F.A₁, ..., F.Aₖ)
```

Here the inner table expression does the grouping and computes all needed aggregate values for each group. The outer SELECT block then evaluates the predicate of the HAVING clause.

Now we show how we can expand an SQL macro for a UDAF A that occurs in a SELECT clause. Such a statement has the following general form:

```
SELECT S1, A(E₁, E₂, ..., Eₙ)
FROM F1
WHERE W1
GROUP BY G1(GA)
HAVING H1 (A₁, ... , Aₖ)
```

The grouping attributes are denoted by GA (which might be an empty set of attributes) and all aggregates in the HAVING clause are denoted by $A_1, \ldots, A_K$. It is possible to transform this statement into the following:

```
SELECT T1.S1, T2.AGGR
FROM (    SELECT S1, GA, A₁, ... , Aₖ
          FROM F1
          WHERE W1
          GROUP BY G1(GA)) AS T1,
      (   SELECT ME1'(E₁, E₂, ..., Eₙ) AS AGGR, GA
          FROM F1, MF1
          WHERE MW1' AND W1
          GROUP BY G1(GA)) AS T2
WHERE H1'(T1.A₁, ... , T1.Aₖ) AND T1.GA = T2.GA
```

In this statement the grouping occurs twice: once to compute the SQL macro and once to compute all other aggregates. This seems to lead to additional work, however, in the query execution plan we can optimize this. For example, it is sufficient to sort the intermediate table F1 only once for both group-by operations.

Expanding SQL Macros that Serve as Restriction

Third, a UDP can be used as a restriction in the WHERE clause of a statement. In this case the output table of the corresponding SQL macro contains a subset of the rows of its input table. The general form of such an SQL macro is the following:

```
SELECT input.*
FROM input, MF1
WHERE MW1
GROUP BY MG1(input.*)
HAVING MH1
```

If a GROUP BY clause is used then *all* columns of the input table must be grouping attributes. A UDP P can occur in the WHERE clause of a statement C. The general form of C is:

```
SELECT S1
FROM F1
WHERE W1 OR (W2 AND P)
GROUP BY G1
HAVING H1
```

Please note that one can transform the WHERE clause always into disjunctive normal form as shown in C above. We can then transform C as follows to expand the SQL macro:

```
SELECT S1
FROM F1
WHERE W1
GROUP BY G1
HAVING H1

UNION

SELECT S1'
FROM (   SELECT F1.* FROM F1, MF1 WHERE MW1'
         GROUP BY MG1'(F1.*) HAVING MH1') AS F
WHERE W2'
GROUP BY G1'
HAVING H1'
```

In summary, we have demonstrated that all statements C that use a UDP as a restriction in their WHERE clause can be transformed in a way that allows the macro expansion.

Expanding SQL Macros that Serve as Join

Finally, an SQL macro can be used to implement a UDP that is used as a join predicate. In this case the output table of the corresponding SQL macro contains a subset of the rows of the Cartesian product of its input tables. The general form of such an SQL macro is the following:

```
SELECT input1.*, input2.*
FROM input1, input2, MF1
WHERE MW1
GROUP BY MG1(input1.*, input2.*)
HAVING MH1
```

Since the statement C has the same form as for UDPs that serve as a restriction, the transformation can be done in the same way.

Expanding SQL Macros in Data Modification Commands

So far we have assumed that the command C is a query. Now we consider the case that C is a data modification command. All UDF in subqueries of data modification commands can be treated with the same rewriting algorithm. This is sufficient for all INSERT commands. Thus, only the cases are left that a UDF is used in the WHERE clause of an UPDATE or DELETE statement or in the SET clause of an UPDATE statement (but not within a subquery). Rewriting can be used in these cases, too, since UPDATE and DELETE statements can be transformed into a representation where UDTO occur only in subqueries. We describe the three rewriting rules using SQL with the extension that we denote primary key attributes by PK. We denote a table by T, an attribute by A, an expression by E and a predicate by P. The first rule allows to transform DELETE statements of the following form:

```
DELETE FROM T
WHERE P( ... UDF ...)
```

This command can be rewritten into the following equivalent command:

```
DELETE FROM T AS T1
WHERE T1.PK IN (SELECT T2.PK FROM T AS T2 WHERE P( ... UDF ...) )
```

UPDATE commands can be rewritten in a similar way. The following command:

```
UPDATE T
SET A = E        .
WHERE P( ... UDF ...)
```

can be transformed into this equivalent statement:

```
UPDATE T AS T1
SET A = E
WHERE T1.PK IN (SELECT T2.PK FROM T AS T2 WHERE P( ... UDF ...) )
```

In the third case, a UDF is used within an expression in the SET clause of an UPDATE statement. The following command:

```
UPDATE T
SET A = E( ... UDF ...)
WHERE P
```

can be transformed into the equivalent statement:

```
UPDATE T AS T1
SET A =          (SELECT E( ... UDF ...)
                 FROM T AS T2
                 WHERE T2. PK = T1.PK)
WHERE P
```

Altogether we have shown that it is always possible to expand SQL macros in SQL DML statements at the textual level by means of equivalence transformations. Hence, a preprocessor can be used to expand SQL macros. Then the modified statement is passed on to the DBMS. As we have already pointed out, SQL macros should not always be used because the traditional implementation by means of an external function might have the better performance in some cases. A preprocessor or an optimizer in the middleware must be aware of this situation and must make a cost-based decision.

7.4 Implementation of Procedural UDTO

In this section, we present the implementation of procedural UDTO. We refer to the implementation within MIDAS that is to a large extent described in [49]. Not all features have been implemented yet: for example, the integration of UDTO into the parallelizer and the new optimizer, Model_M, is still missing. Nevertheless, it is already possible to execute procedural UDTO in parallel (cf. subsection 7.4.4). There are also some restrictions with respect to the body of procedural UDTO: SQL commands referring to input and output tables cannot be used yet. However, one can execute manually crafted gentrees referring to the input and output tables (cf. subsection 7.4.6). While input tables can be referenced multiple times, it is not yet possible to execute more than one insert statement that writes into the output table (cf. subsection 7.4.6). More details on the existing implementation can be found in [49].

In the following subsections, we discuss the extensions that have been made to the different system components to implement procedural UDTO. We begin with the components of the application server and continue with the engine.

7.4.1   Extensions to the SQL Compiler

The CREATE statements for procedural UDTO differ only in their body from those for SQL macros: instead of an INSERT statement the body consists of the keyword EXTERN, the path of a DLL, and the corresponding symbolic entry point. The DROP statement is identical for SQL macros and procedural UDTO. The following is an example for the registration of a procedural UDTO my_udto to MIDAS that has the same functionality as the SQL macro my_macro defined in subsection 7.3.1:

```
CREATE UDTO my_udto
(TABLE my_input (my_id INTEGER, my_text CHAR(*)), my_char CHAR(*) )
RETURNS TABLE my_output (my_id INTEGER, my_text CHAR(*), my_input.+)
AS
EXTERN '/path/udtolib'#'my_input_entry'
```

The signature for procedural UDTO is stored in the system tables in exactly the same way as for SQL macros. However, no gentree for the body is stored in the table sysview. Moreover, the entry type for the UDTO in the table sysfunctions is set to procedural UDTO and the description of the DLL and the entry point are stored there in the same way as for UDSF.

Another difference to SQL macros is that procedural UDTO, same as UDF, cannot be parallelized automatically. Hence, we have defined the ALLOW PARALLEL clause in subsection 6.2.4. The information provided in this clause has to be stored as metadata for parallelization, i.e., we have to store the set of allowed partitioning schemes for the input tables. This information is stored in the table sysfuncimp. Because a procedural UDTO is in a way a black box for the query optimizer, developers should provide hints for the optimizer about the execution costs and the selectivity of a procedural UDTO. In contrast to UDSF it is not sufficient to provide some constant values as parameters for a fixed formula that does the cost computation. Since procedural UDTO are database operators, one can solve both problems as follows (see subsection 7.5.2 for details): the developer provides two functions: one for cost estimation and one for selectivity estimation. Both of these functions are invoked by the optimizer with all statistics that are available for the input tables and the values of the scalar parameters. The use of these statistics makes sense, because UDTO are bulk operators operating on tables.

As the following example statement demonstrates, procedural UDTO may be used exactly in the same way as SQL macros:

```
SELECT * FROM my_udto (systable (segno, tname), 'sys%') a (id, name)
```

In the following, we describe how a procedural UDTO is represented in operator trees of queries and DML statements. A new database operator called udto has been built into the compiler and the execution system of MIDAS. This operator contains - similar to the func node for UDSF - the path and name of the DLL and the entry point for the procedure that implements the body of the procedural UDTO. The udto operator has a variable number of sons, because the number of input tables and scalar parameters varies for different UDTO. Each udto operator has a receive operator as father and send operators as sons. The receive operator reads the output table of the UDTO, the send operators write the input tables. This kind of embedding of udto operators is shown in Figure 37 for a UDTO with two arguments. The reasons for this embedding are: first, the body of the UDTO is always executed by different processes than the surrounding subtrees. Second, the input tables must be materialized if there is more than one reference to them in the body of the UDTO.

Normally send operators have a receive operator as father and vice versa, i.e., they always together as a pair in operator trees. In case of udto operators, the complimentary send and receive operators do not occur explicitly in the operator tree. Rather they are implicitly contained within the udto operator. Hence, the udto operator also stores the needed parameters for the send operator writing to the output tables and for the receive operators reading from the input tables. The udto operator also stores cost informations for the scheduler. However, these costs are not yet computed in MIDAS.

When a DML statement with a procedural UDTO is parsed, the same syntactic and semantic checks are performed as for SQL macros. However, instead of the macro

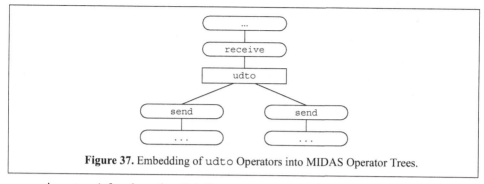

Figure 37. Embedding of udto Operators into MIDAS Operator Trees.

expansion step (cf. subsection 7.3.2) a udto operator is generated with the needed send and receive operators for its embedding. Then the argument trees representing the input tables are placed as inputs for the send operators below the udto operator. The resulting tree with the receive operator as top node is returned to the calling parsing routine.

7.4.2   Extensions to the Optimizer and the Parallelizer

In this subsection, we discuss the necessary extensions for UDTO to Model_M and the parallelizer. Because these extensions have not yet been implemented (extensions for UDSF are also missing for Model_M; see section 2.4 for optimization techniques for them), we present only the concept.

First, the udto operator must be integrated into Model_M as a logical and physical operator. Second, the routines that convert MIDAS operator trees into logical operator trees as input for Model_M and that convert the optimized physical Model_M tree back into a MIDAS operator tree have to be adjusted. Third, the cost model must be extended to UDTO. This includes the invocation of functions for cost and selectivity estimation. Since these functions are provided by developers and are specific for a given UDTO, their description must be retrieved from the system tables. Finally, the rules must be adjusted to take new UDTO into account during transformations. We discuss special optimization rules for UDTO as well as the generation of query execution plans with UDTO as efficient implementations of UDF later in section 7.6.

The extensions to the parallelizer are similar to those for Model_M due to the same underlying technology in both components. For example, a new operator must be defined, the conversion routines and the cost model of the parallelizer must be adapted. Moreover, the rules of the parallelizer manipulating the send and receive operators must take procedural UDTO into consideration. Especially, the allowed partitioning strategies as defined in the ALLOW PARALLEL clause of the CREATE UDTO statement must be considered.

7.4.3   Extensions to the Scheduler

The scheduler breaks an operator tree into subtrees and assigns the subtrees to processing nodes of the parallel machine with the goal to balance the load among the different nodes of the system. The operator tree is normally cut between a `receive` and a `send` operator. Since UDTO embody implicitly the functionality of the `send` operator for the output table and the functionality of the `receive` operators for the input tables, this mechanism has to be adapted: the tree must be cut between the `receive` operator and the `udto` and between the `udto` and its sons, the `send` operators. Thus, a subtree that contains a UDTO with N sons is decomposed into N + 2 subtrees: one subtree containing the `receive` operator as leaf, one subtree containing only the `udto` operator and N subtrees having the sons of the `udto` operator as root. This is demonstrated in Figure 38. Other modifications of the scheduling routines were necessary. For example, the internal identifier of a communication segment (cf. subsection 7.2.2) is normally set by the scheduler when it handles the `send` operator writing to this communication segment. Since there is no send operator for the output table the corresponding routine had to be changed. Another case not occurred before is that the tree is cut immediately below of an operator (the `udto`) having several sons, because a `receive` operator has only a single `send` operator as a son. This results into the situation that one cut creates more than one new subtree. Modifications of the present implementation in order to take care of this special case were necessary, too.

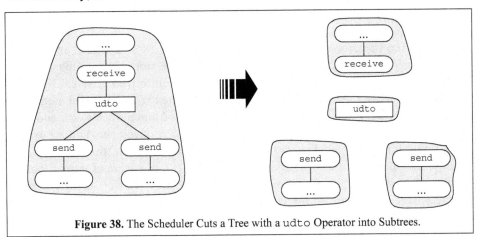

Figure 38. The Scheduler Cuts a Tree with a `udto` Operator into Subtrees.

7.4.4   Extensions to the Execution Engine

Now we present an overview of the execution of UDTO. To simplify the presentation we initially consider only the sequential execution of a QEP with a single `udto` operator.

Figure 39 shows the involved processes of the engine and their interaction during the execution. Application server A processes an SQL statement of an application with a procedural UDTO and translates this statement into a QEP. Then the application server requests a *UDTO_start* process from the segment server (step 1 in Figure 39). Each UDTO_start process has the task to evaluate an instance of a `udto` operator as we will describe below. Each segment server manages a pool of UDTO_start processes on its node. If no free UDTO_start process is available in the pool, the segment server creates a new process, otherwise an existing process is reused (step 2 in Figure 39). The segment server then returns the task ID (that is used for communication by PVM) of the assigned UDTO_start process to the application server A (step 3 in Figure 39).

The application server schedules the QEP as described in subsection 7.4.3. The scheduler assigns the `udto` operator to interpreter A and passes the task ID of the corresponding UDTO_start process to this interpreter (step 4 in Figure 39). The other subtrees of the QEP are assigned to different interpreters not shown in Figure 39. The interpreter passes the `udto` operator to the UDTO_start process (step 5 in Figure

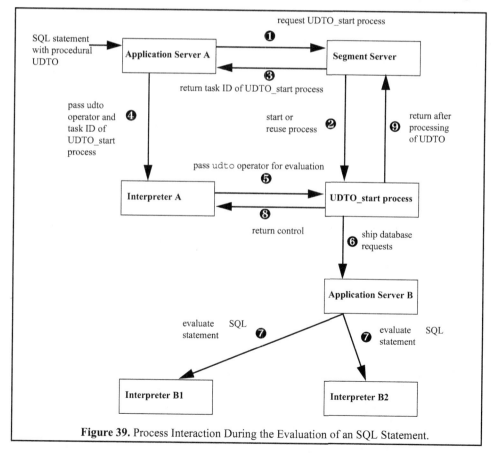

Figure 39. Process Interaction During the Evaluation of an SQL Statement.

39). The UDTO_start process connects via the administration server to a second application server B. It executes the code of the UDTO, i.e., it calls the dynamic linker to link the corresponding DLL to the process and executes the function implementing the body of the UDTO. The UDTO_start process sends all database requests (TBX-commands) that occur within the UDTO body to application server B (step 6 in Figure 39). All of these requests are executed within the same transaction as the QEP that contains the udto operator. This is achieved by means of special extensions to transaction management described below. Complex SQL statements compiled by application server B can be parallelized and executed by several interpreters as usual (this is indicated by the interpreters B1 and B2 for step 7 in Figure 39).

When the evaluation of the UDTO body is finished, the UDTO_start process returns the control to interpreter A (step 8 in Figure 39) and notifies the segment server that it is available to service other requests (step 9 in Figure 39).

In case of a parallel execution of a procedural UDTO, the input tables are partitioned or replicated according to a scheme that the developer has specified (cf. subsection 6.2.4). Copies of the processes interpreter A, UDTO_start process, application server B and the necessary interpreters B_i are needed for each instance of a procedural UDTO. During the parallel execution each instance operates on its partition or copy of an input table and writes to its partition of the output table. Hence, there is no need to synchronize the execution of the different instances with each other. As a result of this architecture, we can now execute a procedural UDTO in parallel by creating several instances and we can also execute the SQL statements within the body of each UDTO instance in parallel.

In the following two subsections, we provide more details on the needed extensions to transaction management and on the implementation of input and output tables.

7.4.5   Extensions to Transaction Management

In this subsection we explain the extensions to transaction management [34] necessary to support our implementation concept for procedural UDTO. As we have already mentioned above, the goal of these extensions was to execute the SQL statements of the UDTO body within the transaction of the QEP which contains this UDTO.

The current transaction concept of MIDAS supports essentially flat ACID transactions (extensions that are beyond the scope of this work can be found in [113]). Normally, there is only one application server that handles all requests of a transaction. This application server is also responsible for transaction management. It generates a unique identifier, the transaction ID, for the transaction and updates data structures for transaction management in the shared memory. This transaction ID is used to link read and write operations with the transaction that caused them. Based on this information, the basic idea for the execution of procedural UDTO is to pass the transaction ID from application server A to application server B (cf. Figure 39) and to use it also to mark all actions that are done by application server B during the execution of the UDTO body. In other words, application server B does not start a new transaction to execute the database commands, but appends its actions to the running transaction of application server A.

Figure 40 shows how this functions in detail. It provides a more detailed view on step 6 of Figure 39. The UDTO_start process gets the transaction ID and the name of the database from application server A through interpreter A. It connects to the database via the administration server and gets the task ID of application server B. Then it passes on to application server B the transaction ID and demands to link all following actions to this transaction. This is done with the new command JOIN TRANSACTION. By contrast, to start a new transaction the command BEGIN TRANSACTION must be used. When all SQL statements are executed, the new command LEAVE TRANSACTION tells application server B to disconnect from the running transaction. This command does not commit the transaction. It is used to reset internal data structures of application server B. Finally, the UDTO_start process disconnects from the database and application server B is free to service other clients.

This concept solves all problems for UDTO related to traditional flat transaction management. However, now multiple DML statements can be executed in parallel within a single transaction. This leads to problems that are similar to those that result from inter-query parallelism within the same transaction (inter-query parallelism is not supported in MIDAS): we have to guarantee that there is no conflict between read and write operations. In case of procedural UDTO the problem is that the statement containing a UDTO is executed in parallel to the statements within the body of the UDTO. The same situation results when procedural UDTO are nested. Moreover, if a statement contains several procedural UDTO then the statements in their bodies are processed in parallel, too.

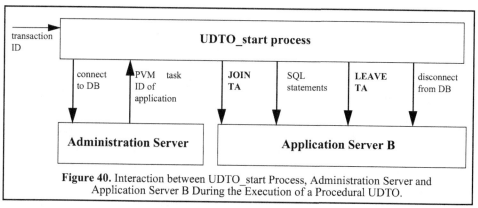

Figure 40. Interaction between UDTO_start Process, Administration Server and Application Server B During the Execution of a Procedural UDTO.

To handle these problems one can employ *intra-transaction synchronization*. The task of intra-transaction synchronization is to prevent conflicts between the different statements. We define that a conflict occurs, if the read sets and the write sets of statements that *might be* executed in parallel overlap. Conflicts must be avoided to guarantee a correct semantics for the statement. Especially, a statement should not see data modified by another statement that might run in parallel. To make this problem more clear, we use a special nested transaction model (cf. [42] and [43] for nested transactions) as a refinement of the ACID-transaction paradigm for the following description. Subtransactions are only used to detect conflicts with respect to intra-transaction synchronization. If a conflict occurs, the statement must be rolled back (statement atomicity), i.e., in contrast to traditional locking protocols, a subtransaction does never wait for a lock.

We demonstrate this problem for a simple example. Figure 41 shows the execution of a statement s1.1 within a transaction T. We assume that s1.1 invokes two procedural UDTO u1 and u2. The body of u1 contains the statements s1.1.1, s1.1.2, ... , s1.1.K, the body of u2 contains the statements s1.2.1, s1.2.2, ... , s1.2.L. Moreover, we assume that the statement s1.2.i invokes a third procedural UDTO u3, which contains the statements s1.2.i.1, s1.2.i.2, ... , s1.2.i.N. The numbers of the statements describe their nesting within the statement s1.1 of transaction T. As shown in Figure 41 JOIN TA and LEAVE TA commands embrace all statements in the bodies of u1, u2, and u3 and integrate them into transaction T. We can now assign the execution of statement s1.1 and of the 3 procedural UDTO to 4 subtransactions: ST1 for statement s1.1, ST1.1 for u1, ST1.2 for u2, ST1.2.i for u3. The numbers of the subtransactions correspond to the prefix of the statement numbers within these subtransactions.

All statements within two different subtransactions can be executed in parallel. We emphasize that this includes parallelism between parent and child subtransactions (for example ST1 and ST1.1) as well as between sibling subtransactions (for exam-

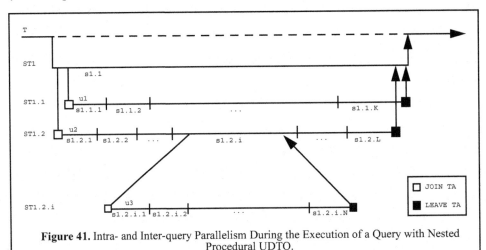

Figure 41. Intra- and Inter-query Parallelism During the Execution of a Query with Nested Procedural UDTO.

ple ST1.1 and ST1.2). Hence, in this example four statements can be executed in parallel as demonstrated in Figure 41. We have to prevent that a subtransaction reads data modified by another subtransaction. However, all statements within the same subtransaction are executed one after the other. Hence, there can be no conflicts within a subtransaction. Please note that the scenario in Figure 41 covers only the sequential execution of the procedural UDTO. In case of a parallel execution there are multiple parallel subtransactions for the execution of each UDTO and there can be also conflicts between them. However, a UDTO should only be executed in parallel if such conflicts do not occur.

How can this kind of intra-transaction synchronization be supported? Traditional concurrency control (or inter-transaction synchronization) is implemented by a hierarchical locking protocol optimized for a high degree of concurrent transactions. By contrast, the most important requirement for intra-transaction synchronization is to operate with low costs. This goal can be achieved by the choice of tables as granule for intra-transaction locks, for example. In this case, if a table has been read by a statement, it cannot be modified by a statement within another subtransaction and vice versa. In addition, if the top-level statement modifies a table, this table must not be updated on the fly and subtransactions have read-only access to it.

We want to point out that intra-transaction synchronization is only needed, if one allows arbitrary data modification statements within the body of procedural UDTO. Of course, INSERT statements that insert into output tables do not cause any conflicts. The same holds for statements that manipulate temporary tables that are created and dropped within each instance of a UDTO. Because in our current view the modification of arbitrary base tables is hardly needed in practical applications, we suggest to allow only data manipulation commands for temporary and output tables (or to leave the responsibility for the correctness to the developer of a UDTO, i.e., the system does not perform any intra-transaction synchronization). In this case, no intra-transaction synchronization is needed. This simplifies the implementation considerably (intra-transaction synchronization is not implemented in MIDAS). We want to remark here that modifications of base tables were not needed in any of the example applications discussed in section 6.3.

7.4.6   Implementation of Input and Output Tables

Now we will describe how input and output tables for procedural UDTO are implemented in MIDAS and how the access to these tables is implemented within the body of procedural UDTO.

Basically, the input tables can be seen as temporary tables that are created and written once and that can be read multiple times. The output table is also a temporary table created once, but there can be several INSERT statements that append tuples to this table. On the other hand, the output table is usually read only once. Only in the case that the output table must be replicated for parallel execution, it is read several times. Both kinds of tables can be created when the evaluation of the UDTO begins and they must exist until this evaluation is finished. The current implementation supports these general requirements. However, optimizations are possible for special cases described later.

The current implementation of both kinds of tables is based on the already existing named communication segments [78]. These communication segments have been introduced to store tables temporarily and remain valid until the end of the transaction. They have a name, which allows to refer to them in other statements. They can be used in operator trees by means of a special implementation of the send and receive operators that get the name of the communication segment as an argument. A send operator may write to a named communication segment and a receive operator may read its input from a named communication segment. The send and the receive operator referring to the same named communication segment may occur in different statements within the same transaction (obviously the send must be executed before the corresponding receive).

Figure 42 shows the use of send and receive operators with names to implement a procedural UDTO with two input tables. The send operators that are the sons of a udto operator and the receive operator on top of a udto work both with named communication segments. Within the body of a UDTO a reference to an input table within an SQL statement is implemented by means of a receive operator that reads from a named communication segment. Conversely, an insertion into the output table is translated into a send operator that writes to the communication segment that is read by the receive on top of the udto. The names that are given to communication segments must be unique within a transaction because they serve as identifiers. Hence, the names that are used for input and output tables are generated by the compiler and are unique for each instance of a udto. Please note that this mechanism is used to transfer both, input tables and scalar UDTO arguments.

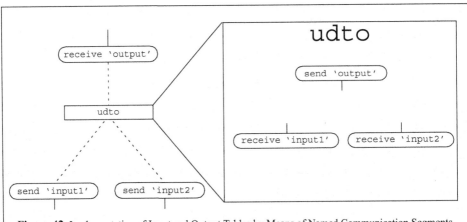

Figure 42. Implementation of Input and Output Tables by Means of Named Communication Segments.

As we have remarked earlier, the implementation is not yet complete. Currently, SQL statements referring to input and output tables cannot be used within the body of UDTO. The reason is that the compiler is not yet extended appropriately. However, it is instead possible to execute a gentree via the TBX interface. Gentrees can refer to input and output tables by using reserved names for the communication segments ('UDTO_input_N' and 'UDTO_output'; N is the number of the input table) that are translated into the correct names for the given udto instance by the compiler.

Moreover, in the current prototype only a single INSERT statement can be executed on the output table. The reason is that communication segments can currently be written only by a single writer, i.e., a single receive operator instance. Possible solutions for this are either to extend the implementation of communication segments appropriately or to modify the compiler as follows[1]: instead of translating different INSERT statements into operator trees with different send operators as root, one may reuse the top send operator that writes into the output table. In this case, the send operator is initialized only once, when the evaluation of the UDTO begins. The operator trees of the different INSERT statements are then appended as subtree to this send operator. If one INSERT has been executed, the subtree is exchanged with that of the next INSERT. We leave it to future work to implement one of these alternatives.

The implementation described above can be enhanced by several measures. We outline these issues here, but they have not been implemented yet. First, the passing of scalar parameters to UDTO can be improved. Currently, scalar parameters are passed on like input tables via a named communication segment. This is a high overhead. Obviously, we can directly pass scalar values on to the UDTO, since their value is known at compile time of the DML statement.

Second, we can optimize the handling of the input tables. If an input table expression with a corresponding QEP q is used only as the input for the UDTO (it could also be a common table expression referenced several times within a query; however this feature is not available in MDAS), then there is a trade-off between the materialization of the input table and its repeated computation, if this is possible. Instead of passing the table to the UDTO, we can also pass the QEP q to the application server that evaluates the embedded SQL statements within the body of the UDTO. Then the application server replaces references to the input table by the QEP, i.e., the input table is derived by the QEP. Since there may be multiple references to this input table within the body of the UDTO, the QEP might be executed several times. In the latter case, it might be better to compute the input table once and materialize it by means of a named communication segment which can then be read several times.

---

1. Proposed by Stephan Zimmermann (private communication).

Third, if an input table is materialized, it may be beneficial to use a communication segment with a B-tree as index. The use of an index is favourable if the input table is accessed multiple times and the index can support these accesses. The difficulty in determining whether materialization and indexing pay off is that the SQL statements are embedded in procedural code, with may include loops and similar constructs. As a result, it is in general impossible to determine how often an embedded SQL statement will be executed. Hence, we cannot automatically predict how often an input table is accessed. A practical work-around for this difficulty might be to allow developers to specify hints for the handling of the input tables (such as materialize or index).

Fourth, the case of a single insertion into the output table can be optimized. Here, one can use pipelining for the communication segment. The pages of the communication segment can then be discarded immediately after they have been read and do not have to be materialized (this is not possible, if the output table must be replicated for parallel execution). This can be implemented in MIDAS by using a usual unnamed instead of a named communication segment.

A final issue concerns the optimization of the implementation of communication segments. Due to the rising importance of symmetric multiprocessors with a shared-memory architecture (the low-end systems with 4 processors are commodity systems now and commodity servers with 8 to 16 processors are expected in the near future), the implementation of communication segments should be optimized for this hardware architecture. This can reduce the costs for communication significantly. The implementation of these five techniques is left to future work. This closes the description of the implementation of procedural UDTO in MIDAS.

7.5 Optimization Issues for UDTO

In this section we want to discuss several technical issues that come along for query optimization with the integration of SQL macros and procedural UDTO into PORDBMS.

7.5.1   UDTO and Implied Predicates

First, we want to discuss an issue that is relevant for query optimization with UDTO. Often, a UDTO that implements a specific UDP A contains one or more additional predicates that are implied by A. Each implied predicate B is always true, if A is true (but usually not vice versa), i.e., $A \rightarrow B$. The reason for the use of implied predicates is that they can be added to implement a cheap filter step. For example, in the SQL macro distance_restriction_1 (cf. subsection 6.3.2) the predicate contains is implied by the predicate internal_distance_less_than. Now the problem with implied predicates is that after the macro expansion they appear in the operator trees together with the original predicate. In this situation a state-of-the-art query optimizer will fail to predict the cardinality of the query result correctly. The reason is that the selectivity of the predicate A AND B is computed as the product of the selectivities of both predicates:

```
sel (A AND B) = sel(A) * sel(B),
```

where `sel()` denotes the selectivity factor of an expression. However, since $A \rightarrow B$ holds, the correct selectivity is the same as the selectivity of A alone, i.e.:

```
sel(A AND B) = sel(A).
```

Similarly, the selectivity of A OR B is the same as the selectivity of B alone, i.e.:

```
sel(A OR B) = sel(B).
```

To the best of our knowledge, there exists no general concept for the treatment of implied predicates during query optimization. This would require interfaces that allow the description of implications between predicates as well as extensions in the optimizer that take implied predicates into account when selectivities are estimated. In the case of UDTO a first, rough solution for the case A AND B would be to assign A the selectivity `sel(A)/sel(B)`. This is correct, since if the restriction with B is done first, then the overall selectivity is computed as `sel(B)*(sel(A)/sel(B))` = `sel(A)`. However, to the best of our knowledge, current systems do not support selectivity specifications as metadata for UDF. Hence, we must provide these selectivity specifications for UDTO that implement restrictions for A and B, respectively. We deal with this issue in the following subsection.

7.5.2   Estimating Costs and Selectivity of UDTO

In this subsection we consider the problem of estimating the selectivity and the execution costs of a UDTO. These values cannot be computed exactly in advance, as there are only estimated statistical descriptions of the input tables and the scalar input parameters of a UDTO. In some cases nothing is known about the input tables and the other parameters. In other cases, for example if an input table is a complete base table, the optimizer can use statistical information from the system catalog tables as a starting point for the cost estimation.

As we have already mentioned before, our general approach to solve the estimation problem is to provide adequate interfaces that allow a developer to register a UDSF for the estimation. In the following, we call this UDSF *estimator*. For each input table or scalar input parameter of the UDTO this estimator needs an input parameter that contains statistical metadata about this UDTO parameter. The statistics are provided by the query optimizer which invokes the estimator. The estimator uses this metadata to compute the cost of the UDTO (which might be actually a cost vector with several components for CPU cost, I/O cost, etc.). This computed cost is then returned to the optimizer as an input for cost-based optimization.

In order to make this feasible, the DBMS must provide data structures with a fixed format to store statistics and cost information. These data structures must then be used to exchange information between the query optimizer and the estimator. Their exact design will depend on the kind of statistics and cost information used by a specific ORDBMS.

This approach is more complicated for developers than the approach for cost computation of UDSF (cf. subsection 2.2.1). However, there is also the advantage that the developer can provide an estimator for the costs that can depend on the value distributions of the input tables. For UDSF one can typically specify only constant costs per UDSF invocation. This cost represents average costs which might be far from accurate for a given query. Especially, if the UDSF is invoked for a large number of rows, the difference between actual costs and average costs can be significant for the overall query processing costs. An obvious example for this is when a UDSF registered with the option NOT NULL call (cf. subsection 2.2.1) is executed on a table with a column containing many NULL values. In this case the UDSF is actually not invoked for all NULL values, but the cost of these invocations is added to the estimated costs of the QEP.

If we want to fully support cost-based query optimization, we have to derive estimated statistics for the output table. These statistics might contain estimates only for the cardinality of the output table (i.e., for the selectivity of the UDTO) or also estimates for the value distributions within its columns. The task to derive estimated statistics for the output table can be solved in the same way as the estimation of the cost of the UDTO: by means of a function that returns the estimated statistics.

This solution should be compared to the state of the art with regard to UDSF. Currently developers of UDSF have no means to control the selectivity estimation for predicates which contain UDSF. There is also no possibility to estimate the value distribution that results from the application of a UDSF. Hence, one should demand that developers get the possibility to register estimation functions for UDSF, too.

We want to add here a remark that concerns the use of UDSF within comparisions. Often a UDF is used within a comparison that compares the UDF result with another expression. An example for this is the predicate `distance(p1, p2) > 50`. This predicate uses the greater-than operator. It is difficult to handle the optimization of such predicates involving user-defined functions because all combinations of comparison operators and UDF must be considered. This task becomes significantly easier, if we rewrite such predicates internally to specialized UDPs that combine the evaluation of a UDF and a comparison, e.g. `distance_greater_than (p1, p2, 50)`. The comparison operator is transformed into a suffix of the UDP (`greater_than`) and the expression is passed on as the last argument to the UDP. This technique provides users with the traditional interface, where comparisons are expressed by the usual comparison operators. On the other hand, the optimizer can invoke estimation routines that perform the selectivity and cost estimation for a specialized UDP.

7.5.3   Application of Traditional Optimization Rules

Rules for pushing-down restrictions and projections were among the first optimization rules for relational query processing. These rules are still very important. Hence, the question arises whether we can also apply them for queries with UDTO.

Our first observation is that these and all other optimization rules may be applied to SQL macros. Since the input tables of an SQL macro may be arbitrary table expressions this can be a significant benefit. The reason is that if a restriction is pushed down through the SQL macro then it may be pushed down further into the QEP of an input table. Hence, it is possible to significantly reduce the cardinality of the input table. Projections can be pushed down in the same manner.

For procedural UDTO the application of push-down optimization rules is in general restricted to the INSERT statements that append tuples to the output table. It is not possible in general to push down restrictions or projections to the input tables, since the effect of the procedural code is not known. However, if a procedural UDTO is used as a high-performance implementation for a UDF operation, we can do better. The reason is that the optimizer knows the effect of the UDTO. For example, if the UDTO serves as an implementation method for a restriction with a UDP then we know that the UDTO is a restriction with some predicate, i.e., its result is a subset of the input tuples. Since the semantics of restrictions is known in advance, we can push-down selections as if the UDTO would be the usual restriction operator that invokes the corresponding UDP. In other words: because the UDTO is simply one implementation alternative, we can perform all optimizations as it would be possible with the traditional implementation by means of an external function. As a conclusion, we see that procedural UDTO as implementation methods should be applied after push-down rules. In this case, all optimizations for restrictions and projections are already accomplished, when the UDTO is considered as an implementation method.

A final optimization is possible that is already used in DB2 UDB for UDTF [50]: if some columns of the output table of a UDTF are not needed for further processing of a statement then one can avoid their production within the body of the UDTF. Since UDTF are always implemented by means of an external function, the optimizer passes to the UDTF a description of the columns actually needed. In case of UDTO the optimizer can automatically add projection operators to the INSERT statements that insert into the output table.

7.6 Using UDTO to Generate Alternative Execution Plans for UDF

This subsection presents an implementation concept for the application of UDTO as high-performance implementations for operations involving UDF. This application was proposed in subsection 6.2.3. The main idea is to extend the rule- and cost-based optimizer of MIDAS (i.e., Model_M) by means of *generic* optimization rules that insert UDTO instead of a traditional operator subtree for UDF into a QEP.

Figure 43 shows an example of such a transformation rule. In this example a UDP serving as a join predicate is evaluated as a restriction on top of a Cartesian product (left side of Figure 43). The transformation rule replaces this subtree by a UDTO that implements a user-defined join algorithm for this predicate (right side of Figure 43). In case of a procedural UDTO a new plan with the udto operator and the necessary send and receive operators is generated. In case of an SQL macro a new plan with an expanded macro is generated. The new operator tree can then be transformed by further rule applications.

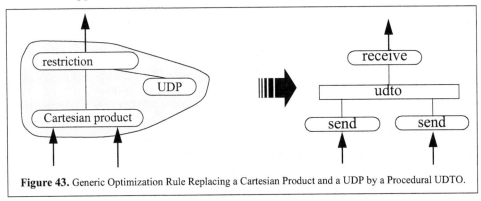

Figure 43. Generic Optimization Rule Replacing a Cartesian Product and a UDP by a Procedural UDTO.

Please note that currently the search engine of Model_M also enumerates Cartesian products. Hence, an operator tree with the subtree shown on the left side of Figure 43 is always generated. If we introduce pruning and do not enumerate all plans that are possible with Cartesian products, the premise of a transformation rule that uses the UDTO might never become true, i.e., the rule is never applied. In this case, the rules of the optimizer must be able to directly introduce a UDTO as a special kind of join, when the join order is changed. This discussion shows that the generic rules generating UDTO as high-performance implementations must fit to the other rules in the rule set. Otherwise, the generic rules for UDTO implementations might not be applicable during the optimization.

Next, we explain how generic transformation rules work. In contrast to other rules, they need information from the system tables to work. Of course, it is not necessary to look up this information each time the rule fires. It is sufficient to read the information when the system is initialized and to notify the optimizer about modifications of the system tables. These generic rules are used to transform operator trees that contain operators with user-defined functionality. In MIDAS these are the func and the udto operator. If one of these operators occurs in the premise of the rule then it will need to check the metadata from the system tables to decide if the rule is actually applicable.

As we have discussed in section 6.3 there can be several UDTO that implement a UDP. In this case, several alternative plans are possible. All these alternatives can be generated by a single rule application, because the Cascades search engine supports rules that have several consequences.

For some generic rules, the subtree representing the consequence of the rule is generated based on information from the system tables. In case of procedural UDTO, only the parameters of the udto operator must be set correctly. However, for SQL macros the macro expansion must be done when the alternative plan is inserted into the memo structure that manages the set of generated operator trees during the optimization. This step is difficult to implement in the MIDAS prototype and will probably also require changes to the search engine. One difficulty is for example that the generic transformation rules work with operator trees that contain logical Cascades operators, while the macro trees are stored as gentrees in the system tables, i.e., as physical MIDAS operator trees. Therefore this extension will need some programming effort.

During the optimization the search engine has to invoke the user-defined estimator functions for costs, selectivity, and value distributions. This is another difference that is caused by the introduction of operators with user-defined functionality: the estimation of the logical and physical properties can be influenced by developers, i.e., parts of the cost model become user-defined.

7.7 Evaluation of the Implementation

The prototypical integration of procedural UDTO into the execution engine of MIDAS has required considerable extensions and some modifications of the existing system. This has been achieved in such a way that changes of existing code were avoided whenever possible. The reason was that we did not want to compromise the stability of the existing system by our implementation.

One drawback of our implementation is the use of several additional processes. To reduce this overhead, one approach could be to integrate procedural UDTO more tightly into the execution system. However, this would increase the complexity of the implementation considerably. Especially, the logic of the application server would become more complex, if only one application server is used. Then the application server must be enabled to execute nested SQL statements, i.e., during the evaluation of a given SQL statement other SQL statements must be parsed and executed. Since procedural UDTO can be nested arbitrarily, the application server must be extended to manage a nested set of SQL statements. For these reasons, we believe that it is better to improve the performance of the system by using threads instead of processes. This approach will reduce the overhead and nevertheless keep the code simple.

Some of the implementation concepts might be reused for commercial ORDBMS, but this largely depends on the existing architecture of commercial systems. Since commercial ORDBMS differ considerably in their architectures from the MIDAS prototype, it is difficult to predict the effort needed to implement UDTO in a given commercial system. However, we believe that this is always possible without major changes of the architecture. The reason is that current commercial PORDBMS should have the key features that were needed to implement UDTO: temporary tables, the use of transaction IDs for transaction management and extensibility of the compiler, the optimizer, and the system tables.

In the following we present some measurements that demonstrate the benefits of SQL macros and procedural UDTO in MIDAS for two applications already described in section 6.3.

7.7.1 Evaluation of SQL Macros

In this section we discuss again the spatial join with the predicate overlaps already introduced in subsections 5.5.1 and 6.3.1. We compare the performance of the following two queries on the table pg2 (cf. subsection 5.5.1):

```
Query 1:
SELECT COUNT(*) FROM pg2 a, pg2 b
WHERE filter_overlaps(a.poly, b.poly) = 1 AND a.id < Num AND b.id < Num

Query 2:
SELECT COUNT(*) FROM
overlaps_d((SELECT id,poly FROM pg2 WHERE id < Num),
           (SELECT id,poly FROM pg2 WHERE id < Num) )
        a (id1,poly1,id2,poly2)
```

Both queries have the parameter Num (number of tuples) that serves to restrict the query to a subset of the table pg2. The first query invokes the function filter_overlaps that is the sophisticated implementation of the UDP overlaps as a UDSF. The resulting query execution plan is exactly the plan B that was described in subsection 5.5.1. The second query explicitly invokes the SQL macro overlaps_d that is similar to the SQL macro proposed in subsection 6.3.1. However, we had to implement the partitioning step differently, because MIDAS does currently not support correlated UDTF. Instead of the UDTF bucket_no we simply used a procedural UDTO. Appendix A.3 shows a visualization of the QEP and the

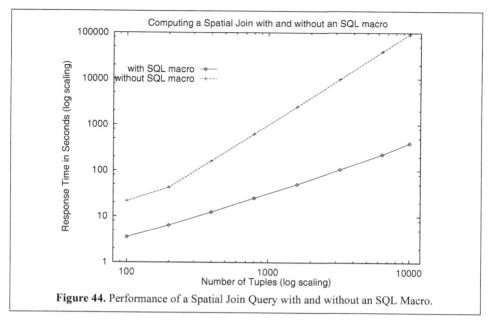

Figure 44. Performance of a Spatial Join Query with and without an SQL Macro.

DDL statements that were used to create the SQL macro and the procedural UDTO. We want to remark here that the SQL macro was optimized by the TransBase optimizer after the expansion. Hence, the resulting plan was slightly different from our manually crafted plan D (cf. subsection 5.5.1). This demonstrates that SQL macro expansion and optimization can seamlessly work together.

Figure 44 shows the response times for the sequential evaluation of the two queries for a varying number of tuples between 100 and 10 000 tuples. The measurements were performed on a 4-processor (each with 100 MHz) SUN SPARC SMP with 128 MB main memory. Obviously, the SQL macro enhances the performance by orders of magnitude: the response time for 10 000 tuples with the SQL macro is 397.4 seconds versus 94 839.2 seconds without the SQL macro. The reason is - as we have already discussed in subsection 5.5.2 - that the asymptotic complexity of the query is $O(N*logN)$ (the selectivity factor of the join predicate is very low), whereas the complexity of the query without the SQL macro is determined by the Cartesian product, i.e., it is $O(N^2)$. These complexities can be directly observed in Figure 44 (please note the log scaling on both axes).

Furthermore, the query containing the SQL macro can be processed in parallel. Actually, the query is already processed in parallel, because the procedural UDTO cut the operator tree into several subtrees by means of send/receive operators. These subtrees are evaluated in parallel. However, the restriction with the exact geometry that accounts for most of the work (cf. subsection 5.5.2) is not processed in parallel. Since the parallelizer has not yet been extended for procedural UDTO, we have parallelized the plan manually in a such way that the restriction is processed by four processes. The response times for the sequential and the parallel execution as well as the speedup are shown in Figure 45. The speedup is well below of the theoretic optimum 4. Several factors contribute to this result: first, as we have already pointed out, the sequential execution already uses some parallelism. Second, the implementation of procedural UDTO (and also of other parts of the execution system) is not fully optimized. Third, we did not use parallel I/O and finally, there was no spare processor to handle the operating system overhead. We would have preferred to conduct the 'sequential' execution on a uniprocessor machine. However, we had no appropriate uniprocessor machine with comparable hardware characteristics for such measurements.

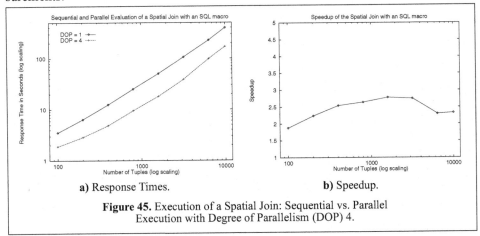

a) Response Times.　　　　　　　　　　b) Speedup.

Figure 45. Execution of a Spatial Join: Sequential vs. Parallel
Execution with Degree of Parallelism (DOP) 4.

7.7.2　Evaluation of Procedural UDTO

In this subsection we demonstrate the benefit of procedural UDTO by means of performance measurements. We have implemented the UDTO median described in subsection 6.3.3 as an example of a procedural UDTO.

Performance measurements were made to compare the performance of the procedural UDTO with the performance of an SQL query without a UDTO that can also be used to compute the median. The query should find the median of the size column in the table parts of the TPC-D benchmark [31]. We have evaluated both queries for a different number of tuples, ranging from 1 000 to 20 000. The measurements were conducted on a 4-processor SUN SPARC SMP with 100 MHz per processor and 128 MB main memory.

The first query with the UDTO median is as follows:

```
SELECT *
FROM median(  (SELECT p_size FROM part
              WHERE p_partkey <= Num) ) m (median)
```

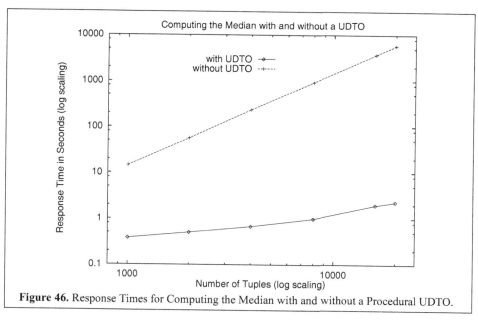

Figure 46. Response Times for Computing the Median with and without a Procedural UDTO.

The parameter `Num` restricts the input table `part` to the desired number of tuples. This holds also for the second query that computes the median via a correlated sub-query as was discussed in subsection 3.4.3.

```
SELECT MIN(p_size)
FROM part l1
WHERE     ( p_partkey <= Num) AND
          ((SELECT (COUNT(*)+1)/2 FROM part WHERE  p_partkey <= Num)
          <=
          (SELECT COUNT(*) FROM part l2 WHERE ( p_partkey <= Num) AND
                 (l2.p_size <= l1.p_size)))
```

The response times are shown in Figure 46. Please note that both axes have a log scaling. We have doubled the number of tuples per query starting with 1 000 until we reached 16 000 and did a final measurement with 20 000 tuples. For the UDTO the execution time rose from 0.38 seconds for 1 000 tuples to 2.3 seconds for 20 000 tuples. This is a very moderate, sublinear increase. The asymptotic complexity of the query is O(N*logN) due to sorting. However, the initial overhead for disk I/O and inter-process communication during the UDTO evaluation is relatively high. For this reason, the response time increases slower for small numbers of tuples.

The response time for the query without the UDTO increases from 14.4 seconds to 5865.0 seconds (roughly 1.6 hours). This steep increase is not surprising since the asymptotic complexity of the query execution plan is $O(N^2)$ because of the corre-lated subquery that is evaluated for each tuple of the outer SELECT block.

As Figure 46 clearly shows, the procedural UDTO enhances the performance by orders of magnitudes. Such dramatic performance gains are always possible when a procedural UDTO lowers the complexity of a query significantly. Because the response times for the query with the procedural UDTO were already small and the overhead for a parallelization is significant in the current implementation, we did not consider parallel execution plans. However, at least for large tables (say a million tuples or more) parallel execution should be an advantage.

7.8 Summary

The goal of the current prototypical implementation was to prove that UDTO can be integrated into a parallel DBMS without a major change of the existing architecture. As the development method was rapid prototyping rather than careful engineering, some reworking and tuning of the implementation still needs to be done. Moreover, some features have yet to be implemented. However, we have reached our goal since the general feasibility was clearly shown. Especially, the implementation of SQL macros could be achieved without major difficulties and should be the first step of an implementation in a commercial DBMS.

An open question is whether the modification of data in base tables should be possible within the body of procedural UDTO. In this case support for intra-transaction synchronization would be needed. However, our exploration of example applications in section 6.3 suggests that there is hardly a need in practical applications.

CHAPTER 8

Summary, Conclusions, and Future Work

In this final chapter we briefly summarize our contributions, draw some general conclusions concerning the design of object-relational (or extensible or generic) DBMS and finish with some remarks on future work.

8.1 Summary

In this work we have made the following main contributions: first, we have proposed new techniques to support data parallelism for UDSF and especially UDAF. For this purpose we have defined extensible execution schemes for UDF and introduced user-defined data partitioning together with a classification of partitioning functions. Second, we have proposed the decompose/compose operator approach to support intra-function parallelism. We have used a pilot implementation on top of a commercial PORDBMS to validate the concept and to show its benefits. Third, the multi-operator paradigm shows that it is possible to implement complex set-oriented operations based on the built-in database operators. Moreover, it demonstrates that applications can sometimes profit from a direct access to the engine via user-defined QEPs. However, the main point is in our view that the multi-operator paradigm was a first step towards UDTO.

Our final and perhaps most important contribution is the design and implementation of UDTO, since this provides extensibility at the level of database operators. Given the fact that set-oriented operations are a core feature of relational database systems, this kind of extensibility is clearly essential. Another view of this is that UDTO push views (SQL macros) and stored procedures (procedural UDTO) into the middle of SQL statements. This enhances the performance of data intensive applications and increases the independence of application code from the implementation of operations on tables. The implementation in the MIDAS prototype proved that UDTO can be integrated into an existing PORDBMS without fundamental changes of the existing architecture.

M. Jaedicke: Parallel Object-Relational Query Processing, LNCS 2169, pp. 145-150, 2001.
© Springer-Verlag Berlin Heidelberg 2001

8.2 Conclusions

The evolution from closed relational database systems to object-relational systems that are open for extensions by third parties is a fundamental change of the field: it is a migration from the fixed relational data model to a fixed object-relational meta ( ) data model. However, this development does not end the discussions on 'the best' data model, since the extensibility of the meta data model is limited. Furthermore, it is not clear what the 'best' meta data model is.

Hence, a fundamental question for the design of extensible DBMS was and still is: how powerful should the extensibility of the system be? In our view the experiences of the last years have taught the following guideline:

> **Do not strive to make the DBMS completely extensible. Instead design algorithms, data structures, and components together with the right set of interfaces in such a way that they are generic, i.e., that third party developers can** *easily* **create a number of useful instances.**

The creation of new instances should be possible by 'simple' programming and the specification of metadata, i.e., without doing 'hard' work with complex, system-specific interfaces and complex dependencies to internal structures. If something is extremely complex to implement for a third party developer, it is probably best to leave this to database vendors. In the following, we support our conclusion by briefly reviewing some examples of ORDBMS techniques:

- Example 1: Generic methods for data items (UDF)

  The basic idea of UDF is to provide the possibility to invoke user-defined code at specific points during query evaluation to allow user-defined computations with attribute values. This allows to extend the DBMS with respect to the operations that are available for data items. The implementation of these functions is not fundamentally different from the implementation of a function in a C or C++ library, for example. However, depending on the DBMS architecture special interfaces for resource allocation and other tasks must be used for the implementation. In addition, metadata is needed to integrate the function fully into query optimization. While UDF offer theoretically unlimited functionality (Turing completeness), they are not suited for all tasks. For example, we have clearly shown that they cannot provide extensibility at the level of database operators.

- Example 2: Generic data containers (LOBs)

  Obviously, extensible DBMS must offer the possibility to store arbitrary new data types. In current ORDBMS, LOBs [63] provide a generic storage facility for data types of nearly unlimited length. LOBs serve as a container to store new data types, but they do not support specific structures for their content. Rather they offer a raw bit string with efficient scan and random access operations. This model is simple, but less generic than the possibility to define structured data types together with optimized storage and access structures. It seems that a simple container model with a simple programming interface and with a highly optimized implementation is a good design.

- Example 3: Generic rule- and cost-based query optimization
  Extensible optimizer technology started with the idea to provide a tool for optimizer generation that allows vendors to quickly construct specialized optimizers. Currently, the state of the art is that vendors implement a single, very complex and sophisticated rule- and cost-based query optimizer with generic optimization rules. These generic rules access the system tables to get information about user-defined extensions. This mechanism offers third party developers a possibility to influence query optimization. We have introduced UDTO to provide the query optimizer with additional strategies for the implementation of operations that involve UDF. This allows to exploit more semantic knowledge about UDF when they are executed within queries.

- Example 4: Generic access operators (Virtual Table Interface and Virtual Index Interface)
  Informix' Virtual Table Interface ([57], [106]) and Virtual Index Interface ([6], [56]) can be seen as interfaces to generic primary and secondary table access operators, respectively. A primary access operator offers the possibility to scan a table and to modify rows. A secondary access operator or index offers a content-based access to rows of a table. Both of these interfaces are complex and their usage requires some expertise due to the inherent dependencies to transaction management services. Nevertheless, the extensibility that these interfaces offer is limited.

- Example 5: Generic search trees (generalized B-trees and Generalized Search Trees)
  Generalized B-trees [102] make B-trees extensible with respect to the data types that can be indexed. This is done by user-defined compare functions that impose an order on instances of a new data type. Generalized Search Trees (GiSTs) [46] are more general in that they allow to implement a specialized search tree, if a hierarchical partitioning of the data set to be indexed exists. However, both are generic tree structures that are limited because they do not allow to implement all kinds of index structures. For example, they cannot implement bit lists or indexes with more than a single indexable data item per attribute or row like traditional full text index structures that index several words per document.

- Example 6: Generic database operators (procedural UDTO and SQL macros)
  We have shown that extensibility with respect to set-oriented operations can be supported by procedural UDTO. They serve as a single generic database operator, whose functionality can be programmed. However, to keep the programming interface simple, the application of procedural UDTO was limited to a subset of row types. SQL macros can be seen as a more convenient way to program new operations, however their expressive power is much more limited.

All these examples do not provide full extensibility in the sense that a DBMS vendor has still more powerful implementation possibilities than a third party developer like an independent software vendor. However, the degree of freedom increases significantly with the introduction of these new techniques. This leads to a more flexible allocation of duties between DBMS vendors and independent software vendors.

As a summary, Figure 47 presents a schematic view of the architecture of PORDBMS as proposed in [13]. As one can observe, all DBMS components (and also the utilities) must be made extensible. Table 10 shows the main components of PORDBMS together with the key techniques that provide extensibility. Due to the

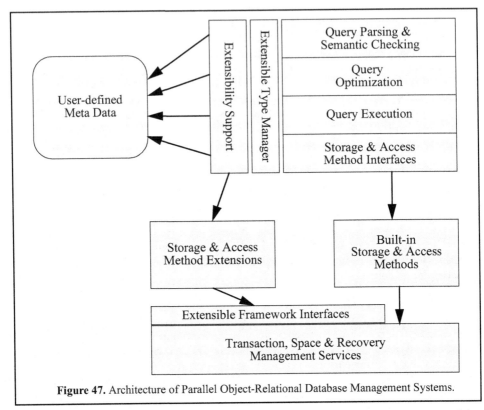

Figure 47. Architecture of Parallel Object-Relational Database Management Systems.

current performance requirements in high-end data management, a competitive ORDBMS must support parallelism for every feature. This includes the features that support extensibility, too.

Table 10. Extensibility for Different DBMS Components by Means of
Generic Data Structures and Algorithms

PORDBMS component	generic data structures and algorithms
parser	driven by system tables
optimizer	rule- and cost-based, generic rules that are driven by system tables (control of rule application, cost and selectivity estimation, SQL macros)
engine	UDF (generic item operations), UDTO (generic database operations)
index manager	Generalized B-Trees, Generalized Search Trees, Virtual Index Interface
storage manager	LOBs with locators, Virtual Table Interface

8.3 Future Work

There is a still a number of open questions in the area of PORDBMS. We want to mention here only some important issues that are directly related to our work. We have grouped these issues around the topics query optimization, user-defined functions and predicates, and user-defined table operators.

Query Optimization

- What pruning strategies are useful for a real-life optimizer based on Cascades?

  Currently, the optimizer (and the parallelizer [80]) of MIDAS use exhaustive search (with respect to the available rule set) in the search engine, which leads to an unacceptable time and space demand for complex queries [62]. Especially the interaction of optimization rules (both transformation and implementation rules) seems to contribute to this problem. These problems deserve careful study. A new version of Cascades, Columbia, with integrated pruning strategies is currently under development at the Portland State University. These new techniques should be explored in the MIDAS optimizer. Moreover, the functionality of the MIDAS optimizer must be completed.

User-Defined Functions and Predicates

- Do we need further optimization rules for UDF?

  As we have mentioned, current PORDBMS support already some generic optimization rules for queries with UDF. Obviously, one question is whether or not further interesting optimization rules exist for UDF.

- How can UDPs be treated as join predicates during join enumeration in optimizers based on System R technology?

  In this work, we have focused on query optimization based on the Cascades optimizer framework. However, many commercial PORDBMS use the optimization technology that was invented for System R. Hence, one should investigate how our techniques can be implemented in this framework.

- How can we support data parallelism for collection data types?

  In chapter 4 we have proposed decompose/compose operators to implement intra-function parallelism. Because collection types can be implemented with LOBs it is promising to explore whether our technique is also useful to parallelize operations on collection data types.

- Are join indexes for UDPs a good idea?

  We have proposed new techniques to define efficient join algorithms for user-defined join predicates. However, some of these predicates are very complex and their evaluation dominates the overall processing time. A possible solution for this problem are join indexes that allow - similar to indexes on UDF - to avoid the evaluation of these expensive predicates during query execution.

User-Defined Table Operators

- What are additional important applications of UDTO?

  We have studied some applications of UDTO. However, we expect that UDTO have a broad applicability. Additional case studies and performance measurements should help to further improve the concept and the implementation.

- Do we need further optimization rules for procedural UDTO?

  We have proposed some optimization rules for projections and restrictions in combination with procedural UDTO. However, there might be other interesting optimization rules.

- Which techniques are useful to optimize the implementation of procedural UDTO further?

  Especially, we can imagine that the management of temporary tables and the access to these tables can be significantly enhanced by indexes. Moreover, special buffer management strategies can be used for their storage.

- Is it useful to generalize UDTO to generic database operators that operate on input tables with arbitrary row types?

  As we have already mentioned such a generalization would increase the flexibility of UDTO further. On the other hand, the implementation of new UDTO becomes more complex.

- Are there other practical approaches to user-defined database operators and especially user-defined joins?

  While we believe that UDTO are a good approach, there might be alternative designs. For example, one could also try to make the existing join operators more generic.

- Do we need run-time optimization for SQL macros?

  Today, most complex queries are compiled at run-time. One advantage of this situation is that the values of parameters are already known when the query is optimized. Hence, it is an interesting question whether dynamic SQL macros should be supported. Dynamic SQL macros would contain several alternative implementations from which they choose at run-time the best one. This decision should be based on the actual statistics for the input tables and the values of the scalar parameters.

- Should the next generation of DBMS engines be built with a different kind of operators?

  The optimization of complex object-relational queries is difficult due to the large number of parameters that can be only estimated at compile time. As a result, it might be desirable to compute aggregates and statistics during the execution of an operator and to pass this information to the next operator. The next operator could then use this up-to-date information to choose the best available algorithm for its execution. One could also dynamically change the execution order of the operators, i.e., the structure of the operator tree. The disadvantage of this execution model is that it does not support pipelining. Hence, the delivery of the first tuple might be delayed significantly.

References

Abbreviations

ACM	Association for Computing Maschinery
BTW	Conference Datenbanksysteme in Büro, Technik und Wissenschaft
CACM	Communications of the ACM
DASFAA	International Conference on Database Systems for Advanced Applications
EDBT	International Conference on Extending Database Technology
ICDE	International Conference on Data Engineering
IDEAS	International Database Engineering & Applications Symposium
IEEE	Institute of Electrical and Electronics Engineers
LNCS	Lecture Notes in Computer Science (Springer)
PDIS	International Conference on Parallel and Distributed Information Systems
PODS	ACM Symposium on Principles of Database Systems
SIGMOD	ACM SIGMOD International Conference on Management of Data
TKDE	IEEE Transactions on Knowledge and Data Engineering
TODS	ACM Transactions on Database Systems
VLDB	International Conference on Very Large Data Bases

[1]   Agrawal, R., Mannila, H., Srikant, R., Toivonen, H., Verkamo, A.: Fast Discovery of Association Rules. Advances in Knowledge Discovery and Data Mining 1996: 307-328.

[2]   Amdahl, G. M.: Validity of Single_processor Approach to Achieving Large-Scale Computing Capability, Proc. AFIPS Conf., 1967: 483-485.

[3]   Antoshenkov, G., Ziauddin, G.: Query Processing and Optimization in Oracle Rdb. VLDB Journal 5(4): 229-237 (1996).

[4]   Apers, P. M. G., van den Berg, C. A., Flokstra, J., Grefen, P. W. P. J., Kersten, M. L., Wilschut, A. N.: PRISMA/DB: A Parallel Main Memory Relational DBMS. TKDE 4(6): 541-554 (1992).

[5]   Billings, K.: A TPC-D Model for Database Query Optimization in Cascades, Master Thesis, Portland State Universisty, CS department, 1997.

[6]   Bliujute, R., Saltenis, S., Slivinskas, G., Jensen, C. S.: Developing a DataBlade for a New Index, A TIMECENTER Technical Report, TR-29, http://www.cs.auc.dk/research/DBS/tdb/TimeCenter/, 1998.

152   References

[7]   Bozas, G.: Scalability in Parallel Database Systems, Ph.D. Thesis, Fakultät für Informatik, Technische Universität München, 1998.

[8]   Bozas, G., Fleischhauer, M., Zimmermann, S.: PVM Experiences in Developing the MIDAS Parallel Database System, Proceedings of the 4th European PVM User Group Meeting - EuroPVM'97, Krakow, Poland, November 1997.

[9]   Bozas, G., Jaedicke, M., Listl, A., Mitschang, B., Reiser, A., Zimmermann, S.: On Transforming a Sequential SQL-DBMS into a Parallel One: First Results and Experiences of the MIDAS-Project, Proc. of 2nd Int. Euro-Par Conf., LNCS 1123, Springer, 1996.

[10]   Brandmayer, F.: Parallel Query Execution in MIDAS (in German), Master Thesis, Institut für Informatik, Technische Universität München, 1997.

[11]   Brinkhoff, T., Kriegel, H.-P., Schneider, R., Seeger, B.: Multi-Step Processing of Spatial Joins. SIGMOD Conf. 1994: 197-208.

[12]   Carey, M. J., Dewitt, D. J.: Of Objects and Databases: A Decade of Turmoil, VLDB 1996.

[13]   Carey, M. J., Mattos, N., Nori, A.: Object-Relational Database Systems: Principles, Products, and Challenges (Tutorial). SIGMOD 1997: 502.

[14]   Carey, M. J., DeWitt, D.J., Graefe, G., Haight, D. M., Richardson, J. E., Schuh, D. T., Shekita, E. J., Vandenberg, S. L.: The EXODUS Extensible DBMS Project: An Overview, in: Zdonik, S., Maier, D. (eds.): Readings in Object-Oriented Databases, Morgan-Kaufmann, 1990.

[15]   Chamberlin, D.: A Complete Guide to DB2 Universal Database, Morgan Kaufman Publishers, San Francisco, 1998.

[16]   Chatziantoniou, D., Ross, K. A.: Groupwise Processing of Relational Queries. VLDB 1997: 476-485.

[17]   Chaudhuri, S., Shim, K.: Optimization of Queries with User-defined Predicates. VLDB 1996: 87-98.

[18]   Clausnitzer, A., Jaedicke, M., Mitschang, B., Nippl, C., Reiser, A., Zimmermann, S.: On the Application of Parallel Database Technology for Large Scale Document Management Systems. IDEAS 1997: 388-396.

[19]   Davis, J. R.: Creating an extensible, Object-Relational Data Management Environment: IBM's Universal Database, White Paper, Database Associates International,1996.

[20]   Deßloch, S., Härder, T., Mattos, N., Mitschang, B., Thomas, J.: Advanced Data Processing in KRISYS: Modeling Concepts, Implementation Techniques, and Client/Server Issues. VLDB Journal 7(2): 79-95 (1998).

[21]   Deßloch, S., Mattos, N.: Integrating SQL Databases with Content-Specific Search Engines. VLDB 1997: 528-537.

[22]   DeWitt, D., Gray, J.: Parallel Database Systems: The Future of High Performance Database Systems, CACM, Vol.35, No.6, 85-98, 1992.

[23]   DeWitt, D.: Parallel Object-Relational Database Systems: Challenges & Opportunities, invited talk, PDIS 1996.

[24]   DeWitt, D. J., Carey, M., Naughton, J., Asgarian, M., Gehrke, J., Shah, D.: The BUCKY Object-Relational Benchmark, SIGMOD 1997: 135-146.

[25]   Elhardt, K., Killer, D., Lehnert, K., Seibt, C.: The Database System MERKUR, Technical Report TUM-I8702, Institut für Informatik, Technische Universität München, Februray 1987.

[26]   Fleischhauer, M.: Parallelization of Relational Database Queries in MIDAS (in German), Master Thesis, Institut für Informatik, Technische Universität München, 1997.

[27]   Geist, A., Beguelin, A., Dongarra, J., Jiang, W., Manchek, R., Sunderam, V.: PVM: Parallel Virtual Machine - A Users' Guide and Tutorial for Network Parallel Computing, The MIT Press, 1994.

[28]   Gesmann, M.: A Cost Model for Parallel Navigational Access in Complex-Object DBMSs. DASFAA 1997: 1-10.

[29]   Graefe, G.: Query Evaluation Techniques for Large Databases. Computing Surveys 25(2): 73-170 (1993).

[30] Graefe, G.: The Cascades Framework for Query Optimization. Data Engineering Bulletin 18(3): 19-29 (1995).

[31] Gray, J. (editor): The Benchmark Handbook for Database and Transaction Processing Systems, Morgan Kaufmann, San Francisco, 1993.

[32] Gray, J.: A Survey of Parallel Database Techniques and Systems, Tutorial Handout at VLDB 1995.

[33] Gray, J., Chaudhuri, S., Bosworth, A., Layman, A., Reichart, D., Venkatrao, M., Pellow, F., Pirahesh, H.: Data Cube: A Relational Aggregation Operator Generalizing Group-By, Cross-Tab, and Sub-Totals, Data Mining and Knowledge Discovery 1, Kluwer Academic Publishers, 1997: 29-53.

[34] Gray, J., Reuter, A.: Transaction Processing: Concepts and Techniques, Morgan Kaufman Publishers, 1993.

[35] Güting, R. H.: Second-Order Signature: A Tool for Specifying Data Models, Query Processing, and Optimization, SIGMOD Conference 1993: 277-286.

[36] Haas, L. M., Freytag, J.C., Lohman, G. M., Pirahesh, H.: Extensible Query Processing in Starburst. SIGMOD 1989: 377-388.

[37] Haas, L. M., Chang, W., Lohman, G. M., McPherson, J., Wilms, P. F., Lapis, G., Lindsay, B. G., Pirahesh, H., Carey, M. J., Shekita, E. J.: Starburst Mid-Flight: As the Dust Clears. TKDE 2(1): 143-160 (1990).

[38] Haas, L. M., Kossmann, D., Wimmers, E. L., Yang, J.: Optimizing Queries Across Diverse Data Sources. VLDB 1997: 276-285.

[39] Haas, S.: Extension of the SQL-Parser of MIDAS by User-Defined Functions (in German), System Development Project, Institut für Informatik, Technische Universität München, 1998.

[40] Härder, T., Meyer-Wegener, K., Mitschang, B., Sikeler, A.: PRIMA - a DBMS Prototype Supporting Engineering Applications. VLDB 1987: 433-442.

[41] Härder, T., Rahm, E.: Data Base Systems - Concepts and Techniques for their Implementation (in German), Springer, 1999.

[42] Härder, T., Rothermel, K.: Concurrency Control Issues in Nested Transactions. VLDB Journal 2(1): 39-74 (1993).

[43] Härder, T., Rothermel, K.: Concepts for Transaction Recovery in Nested Transactions. SIGMOD Conference 1987: 239-248.

[44] Hahn, K., Seehafer, R.: Intra-Function Parallelism in ORDBMS (in German), System Development Project, Institut für Informatik, Technische Universität München, 1998.

[45] Hellerstein, J. M., Stonebraker, M.: Predicate Migration: Optimizing Queries with Expensive Predicates. SIGMOD 1993: 267-276.

[46] Hellerstein, J. M., Naughton, J. F., Pfeffer, A.: Generalized Search Trees for Database Systems. VLDB 1995: 562-573.

[47] Hellerstein, J. M., Naughton, J. F.: Query Execution Techniques for Caching Expensive Methods. SIGMOD 1996: 423-434.

[48] Hilbig, M.: Development of a Cost-based Query Optimizer for the Parallel Relational Database System MIDAS (in German), Master Thesis, Institut für Informatik, Technische Universität München, 1998.

[49] Heupel, S.: Implementation of Extensible Database Operators in a Parallel, Object-Relational Database System (in German), Master Thesis, Institut für Informatik, Technische Universität München, 1998.

[50] IBM DB2 Universal Database SQL Reference, Version 5, Document Number: S10J-8165-00, 1997.

[51] IBM DB2 Universal Database, Embedded SQL Programming Guide, Version 5, Document Number: S10J-8158-00, 1997.

[52] IBM DB2 Universal Database Text Extender, Administration and Programming, Document Number: SC26-9108-00, 1997.

[53] Illustra User's Guide, Illustra Information Technologies, Inc., 1995.

[54] Informix Universal Server, DataBlade API Programmer's Manual Vers. 9.12, Informix Software Inc., 1997.

[55] Informix Universal Server, DataBlade Developer's Kit User's Guide, Version 3.4, Informix Software Inc.

[56] Informix Universal Server, Virtual-Index Interface Programmer's Manual, Vers. 9.1, Informix Software Inc., 1997.

[57] Informix Universal Server, Guide to the Virtual Table Interface, Vers. 9.0, Informix Software Inc., 1996.

[58] Informix Web DataBlade Module, Users's Guide, Version 3.3., Informix Software Inc., 1997.

[59] Jaedicke, M., Mitschang, B.: A Framework for Parallel Processing of Aggregate and Scalar Functions in Object-Relational DBMS, TUM-I 9741, SFB-Bericht Nr. 342/25/97 A, September 1997. (http://www3.informatik.tu-muenchen.de/public/projekte/sfb342/publications.html).

[60] Jaedicke, M., Mitschang, B.: On Parallel Processing of Aggregate and Scalar Functions in Object-Relational DBMS, SIGMOD 1998: 379-389.

[61] Jaedicke, M., Mitschang, B.: User-Defined Table Operators: Enhancing Extensibility for ORDBMS, to appear at VLDB 1999.

[62] Krueger-Barvels, K.: Development of a Rule-based Query Optimizer for the Parallel Object-Relational Database System MIDAS (in German), Master Thesis, Institut für Informatik, Technische Universität München, 1998.

[63] Lehman, T. J., Gainer, P.: DB2 LOBs: The Teenage Years. ICDE 1996: 192-199.

[64] Lehn, R., Bayer, R.: Parallelization of Profiling Services, internal report, Fakultät für Informatik, Technische Universität München, 1994.

[65] Listl, A., Bozas, G.: Performance Gains Using Subpages for Cache Coherency Control, Proceedings of the 8th International Workshop on Database and Expert Systems Applications, Toulouse, France, 1997.

[66] Listl, A., Pawlowski, M., Reiser, A., Bozas, G., Lehn, R.: Architecture of the Parallel Database System MIDAS (in German). BTW'95, Dresden, 1995: 252-261.

[67] Lohman, G. M.: Grammar-like Functional Rules for Representing Query Optimization Alternatives. SIGMOD 1988: 18-27.

[68] Lohman, G. M., Lindsay, B. G., Pirahesh, H., Schiefer, K. B.: Extensions to Starburst: Objects, Types, Functions, and Rules. CACM, Vol. 34, No. 10, 1991: 94-109.

[69] Mattos, N.: An Overview of the SQL3 Standard, Database Technology Institute, IBM Santa Teresa Lab, San Jose, California, 1996.

[70] Mattos, N., Deßloch, S., DeMichiel, L., Carey, M.: Object-Relational DB2, IBM White Paper, July 1996.

[71] McKenna, W. J., Burger, L., Hoang, C., Truong, M.: EROC: A Toolkit for Building NEATO Query Optimizers. VLDB 1996: 111-121.

[72] Mishra, P., Eich, M. H.: Join Processing in Relational Databases. Computing Surveys 24(1): 63-113 (1992).

[73] Mitschang, B.: Query Processing in Database Systems (in German), Vieweg, 1995.

[74] Mitschang, B., Pirahesh, H., Pistor, P., Lindsay, B. G., Südkamp, N.: SQL/XNF - Processing Composite Objects as Abstractions over Relational Data. ICDE 1993: 272-282.

[75] Näher, S., Uhrig, C.: The LEDA User Manual, Version R 3.5, 1997 (http://www.mpi-sb.mpg.de/LEDA/leda.html).

[76] Ng, W., Levene, M.: OSQL: An Extension to SQL to Manipulate Ordered Relational Databases. IDEAS 1997: 358-367.

[77] Niblack, W., Barber, R., Equitz, W., Flickner, M., Glasman, E. H., Petkovic, D., Yanker, P., Faloutsos, C., Taubin, G.: The QBIC Project: Querying Images by Content, Using Color, Texture, and Shape. Storage and Retrieval for Image and Video Databases (SPIE) 1993: 173-187.

[78] Nippl, C.: Ph.D. Thesis in preparation, Fakultät für Informatik, Technische Universität München, to appear 1999.

[79] Nippl, C., Jaedicke, M., Mitschang, B.: Accelerating Profiling Services by Parallel Database Technology. Proceedings of the International Conference on Parallel and Distributed Processing Techniques and Applications (PDPTA), Las Vegas, Nevada, July 1997.

[80] Nippl, C., Mitschang, B.: TOPAZ: a Cost-Based, Rule-Driven, Multi-Phase Parallelizer, VLDB 1998: 251-262.

[81] Nori, A., Kumar, S.: Bringing Objects to the Mainstream, Proceedings of the 1997 COMPCON Conference, 1997: 136-142.

[82] O'Connell, W., Carino, F., Linderman, G.: Optimizer and Parallel Engine Extensions for Handling Expensive Methods Based on Large Objects, Technical Report, NCR Teradata Database Engineering, Parallel Systems, 1998.

[83] O'Connell, W., Ieong, I.T., Schrader, D., Watson, C., Au, G., Biliris, A., Choo, S., Colin, P., Linderman, G., Panagos, E., Wang, J., Walters, T.: Prospector: A Content-Based Multimedia Server for Massively Parallel Architectures. SIGMOD 1996: 68-78.

[84] Olson, M. A.: DataBlade Extensions for INFORMIX-Universal Server, Proceedings of the 1997 COMPCON Conference, 1997: 143-148.

[85] Olson, M. A., Hong, W. M., Ubell, M., Stonebraker, M.: Query Processing in a Parallel Object-Relational Database System, Data Engineering Bulletin 19(4): 3-10 (1996).

[86] Oracle 8, Manuals, Oracle Corporation, 1998.

[87] Orenstein, J. A.: A Comparison of Spatial Query Processing Techniques for Native and Parameter Spaces. SIGMOD 1990: 343-352.

[88] Patel, J. M., DeWitt, D. J.: Partition Based Spatial-Merge Join. SIGMOD 1996: 259-270.

[89] Patel, J., Yu, J. Kabra, N., Tufte, K., Nag, B., Burger, J., Hall, N., Ramasamy, K., Lueder, R., Ellman, C., Kupsch, J., Guo, S., DeWitt, D. J., Naughton, J.: Building A Scalable GeoSpatial Database System: Technology, Implementation, and Evaluation, SIGMOD 1997: 336-347

[90] Perathoner, S.: Extending the MIDAS System Tables with Statistics and Object-Relational Functionality (in German), System Development Project, Institut für Informatik, Technische Universität München, 1998.

[91] Perathoner, S.: Development of a Component for Load Balancing for the Parallel Database System MIDAS (in German), Master Thesis, Institut für Informatik, Technische Universität München, 1998.

[92] Pfoser, D., Jensen, C. S.: Incremental Join of Time-Oriented Data, A TIMECENTER Technical Report, TR-34, http://www.cs.auc.dk/research/DBS/tdb/TimeCenter/, 1998.

[93] Pirahesh, H., Mitschang, B., Südkamp, N., Lindsay, B. G.: Composite-Object Views in Relational DBMS: An Implementation Perspective. EDBT 1994: 23-30.

[94] Red Brick Systems, Inc., http://www.redbrick.com/rbs-g/html/whpap.html, August 1997.

[95] Roy, J.: Aggregations in the Environment of Informix Dynamic Server with Universal Data Option. Informix Tech Notes, Volume 8, Issue 2, Informix Software Inc., 1998.

[96] Saracco, C. M.: Universal Database Management. A Guide to Object/Relational Technology, Morgan Kaufmann Publishers, 1998.

[97] Sarawagi, S., Thomas, S., Agrawal, R.: Integrating Mining with Relational Database Systems: Alternatives and Implications. SIGMOD 1998: 343-354.

[98] Seshadri, P., Livny, M., Ramakrishnan, R.: The Case for Enhanced Abstract Data Types. VLDB 1997: 66-75.

[99] Shatdal, A., Naughton, J. F.: Adaptive Parallel Aggregation Algorithms. SIGMOD 1995: 104-114.

[100] SFB 342: Tools and Methods for the Utilization of Parallel Computer Architectures (in German), Work and Result Report 1995/1996/1997, Technische Universität München, 1997.

[101] SQL Multimedia and Application Packages (SQL/MM), ISO Working Draft, ISO/IEC JTC1/SC21 Information Retrieval, Transfer and Management for OSI WG3 Database, March 1996.

[102] Stonebraker, M.: Inclusion of New Types in Relational Data Base Systems. ICDE 1986: 262-269.

[103] Stonebraker, M.: The Case for Shared Nothing. Database Engineering Bulletin 9(1), 1986: 4-9.

[104] Stonebraker, M., Moore, D.: Object-Relational DBMSs - The Next Great Wave, Morgan Kaufman Publishers, 1996.

[105] Stonebraker, M.: Implementation of Integrity Constraints and Views by Query Modification. SIGMOD Conference 1975: 65-78.

[106] Stonebraker, M., Brown, P., Herbach, M.: Interoperability, Distributed Applications and Distributed Databases: The Virtual Table Interface. Data Engineering Bulletin 21(3), 1998: 25-33.

[107] Stonebraker, M., Frew, J., Gardels, K., Meredith, J.: The Sequoia 2000 Benchmark. SIGMOD 1993: 2-11.

[108] Stonebraker, M., Rowe, L. A., Hirohama, M.: The Implementation of Postgres. TKDE 2(1), 1990: 125-142.

[109] TransBase Relational Database System, Version 3.3, System Guide, TransAction Software GmbH, München, 1988.

[110] Valduriez, P.: Parallel Database Systems: Open Problems and New Issues, in: Distributed and Parallel Databases, Vol.1, No. 2, April 1993, 137-166.

[111] Yan, W. P., Larson, P.: Eager Aggregation and Lazy Aggregation. VLDB 1995: 345-357.

[112] Zhou, X., Abel, D. J., Truffet, D.: Data Partitioning for Parallel Spatial Join Processing. SSD 1997: 178-196.

[113] Zimmermann, S.: Ph.D. Thesis in preparation, Fakultät für Informatik, Technische Universität München, to appear 2000.

Appendix A

A.1 The Program `sequential_invert`

The following is a simplified version of the program `sequential_invert` that was used in section 4.3.

```
EXEC SQL INCLUDE SQLCA;

void main()
{
// declare host variables
EXEC SQL BEGIN DECLARE SECTION;
    SQL TYPE IS CLOB_LOCATOR clob;
 ...
EXEC SQL END DECLARE SECTION;

EXEC SQL WHENEVER SQLERROR GO TO badnews;
EXEC SQL CONNECT TO test;

//    declare a cursor for the query
EXEC SQL DECLARE c2 CURSOR FOR
select id, invert(text,1,1) from clobtable;

// open cursor
EXEC SQL OPEN c2;

EXEC SQL WHENEVER NOT FOUND GOTO exit;

// fetch all tuples and insert them into table result
while(1 )
{
    EXEC SQL FETCH c2 INTO :no, :clob;
    EXEC SQL INSERT INTO result values (:no , :clob);
}

exit:
EXEC SQL ROLLBACK;
```

M. Jaedicke: Parallel Object-Relational Query Processing, LNCS 2169, pp. 157-161, 2001.
© Springer-Verlag Berlin Heidelberg 2001

```
EXEC SQL CONNECT RESET;
return;

badnews:
// error handling ...
}
```

A.2 The Program parallel_invert

The following program listing is a simplified version of the program
parallel_invert that was used in section 4.3. The query that is associated with
cursor c2 is executed in parallel by DB2. Please note that in DB2 UDB the default
degree of parallelism of SQL statements can be set to a specific value by assigning
this value to the parameter DEGREE, when the program is bound to the database. DB2
tries to use this default degree of parallelism, whenever possible. Otherwise DB2
chooses a smaller degree of parallelism. For example, the INSERT statements in the
following program can be executed only with a degree of parallelism one, i.e., in a
sequential manner, because only one row is inserted.

```
EXEC SQL INCLUDE SQLCA;
void main()
{
// declare host variables
EXEC SQL BEGIN DECLARE SECTION;
     SQL TYPE IS CLOB_LOCATOR clob;
     SQL TYPE IS CLOB_LOCATOR clob2;
     long no;
     long tmpno;
     long part;
EXEC SQL END DECLARE SECTION;

EXEC SQL WHENEVER SQLERROR GO TO badnews;
EXEC SQL CONNECT TO test;

// declare a cursor for the query
// join with jointable serves to copy LOB locators (DECOMPOSE step)
// the value of N is the constant 4, the value of K is given by b.id2
EXEC SQL DECLARE c2 CURSOR FOR
Select a.id + 0 as id1, b.id2 + 0 as id2, invert(a.text, b.id2, 4) as text
from clobtable as a, jointable as b where a.id=b.id1 order by id1, id2;

// open cursor
EXEC SQL OPEN c2;
```

```
EXEC SQL WHENEVER NOT FOUND GOTO exit;
tmpno = 0;

while(1)
{
        // fetch next result pieces
        EXEC SQL FETCH c2 INTO :no, :part, :clob;
        if(tmpno==0) tmpno = no;

        if(tmpno != no)
        { // first piece of a different CLOB is fetched:
          // insert composed CLOB into table result
          // and free its locator
          EXEC SQL INSERT INTO result values (:tmpno , :clob2);
          EXEC SQL FREE LOCATOR :clob2;
            tmpno = no;
        }

        // COMPOSE step
        if(part == 1)                //first piece of a CLOB
            EXEC SQL VALUES :clob INTO :clob2;
        else                         // second and further pieces
          EXEC SQL VALUES :clob2 || :clob INTO :clob2;
}

exit:
// insert last composed CLOB into table result and free its locator
EXEC SQL INSERT INTO result values (:tmpno, :clob2);
EXEC SQL FREE LOCATOR :clob2;

EXEC SQL ROLLBACK;
EXEC SQL CONNECT RESET;
return;

badnews:
    // error handling ...
} )
```

A.3 The Query Execution Plan for the Spatial Join with SQL Macro

The figure on the following page shows a visualization of the gentree for the spatial join described in subsection 7.7.1. The query execution plan was produced for the following query with the SQL macro overlaps_d:

```
SELECT COUNT(*) FROM
overlaps_d((SELECT id,poly FROM pg2 WHERE id < 100),
            (SELECT id,poly FROM pg2 WHERE id < 100) )
         a (id1,poly1,id2,poly2)
```

The SQL macro `overlaps_d` was defined as follows:

```
CREATE UDTO overlaps_d
(TABLE ovl_dinput1(id1 INTEGER, poly1 CHAR(*)),
 TABLE ovl_dinput2(id2 INTEGER, poly2 CHAR(*)) )
RETURNS TABLE ovl_doutput1(id1 INTEGER, poly1 CHAR(*), ovl_dinput1.+,
         id2 integer, poly2 CHAR(*), ovl_dinput2.+)
AS
INSERT INTO ovl_doutput1
SELECT c.id1, d.poly1, ovl_dinput1.+, c.id2, e.poly2, ovl_dinput2.+
FROM   (SELECT DISTINCT a.id, b.id
        FROM bucket_no ( (SELECT s.id1, pg_bbox(s.poly1)
                          FROM ovl_dinput1 s) ) a (id, bbox, bno),
              bucket_no ( (SELECT t.id2, pg_bbox(t.poly2)
                          FROM ovl_dinput2 t) ) b (id, bbox, bno)
        WHERE a.bno = b.bno AND
              bbox_overlaps(a.bbox, b.bbox) = 1)
        c (id1, id2), ovl_dinput1 d, ovl_dinput2 e
WHERE c.id1 = d.id1 AND c.id2 = e.id2 AND
      pg_overlaps(d.poly1, e.poly2) = 1
```

The procedural UDTO `bucket_no` was registered with MIDAS by means of the statement:

```
CREATE UDTO bucket_no (TABLE bucket_no_in(id INTEGER,poly CHAR(*)))
RETURNS TABLE bucket_no_out (id INTEGER,bbox CHAR(*), bucketno INTEGER)
AS
EXTERN
'/nfs/sunbayer63/home/wiss/jaedicke/mylibs/libudto.so'#'bucket_no'
```

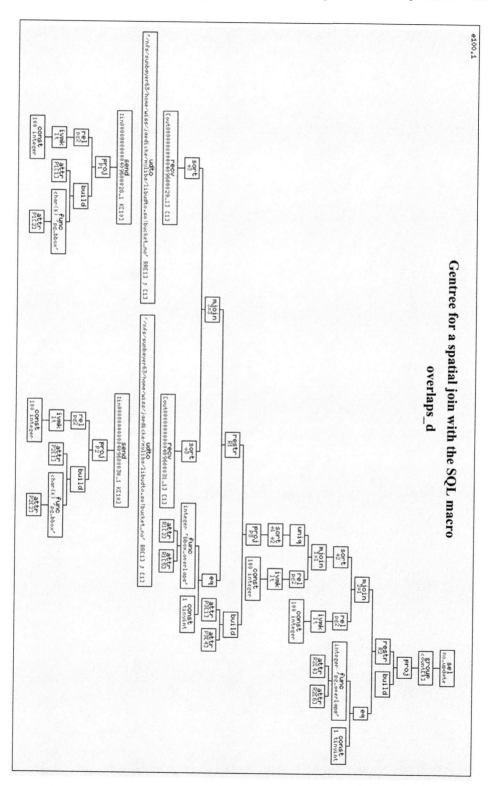

Gentree for a spatial join with the SQL macro overlaps_d

Lecture Notes in Computer Science

For information about Vols. 1–2130
please contact your bookseller or Springer-Verlag

Vol. 2168: L. De Raedt, A. Siebes (Eds.), Principles of Data Mining and Knowledge Discovery. Proceedings, 2001. XVII, 510 pages. 2001. (Subseries LNAI).

Vol. 2169: M. Jaedicke, New Concepts for Parallel Object-Relational Query Processing. XI, 161 pages. 2001.

Vol. 2170: S. Palazzo (Ed.), Evolutionary Trends of the Internet. Proceedings, 2001. XIII, 722 pages. 2001.

Vol. 2172: C. Batini, F. Giunchiglia, P. Giorgini, M. Mecella (Eds.), Cooperative Information Systems. Proceedings, 2001. XI, 450 pages. 2001.

Vol. 2173: T. Eiter, W. Faber, M. Truszczynski (Eds.), Logic Programming and Nonmonotonic Reasoning. Proceedings, 2001. XI, 444 pages. 2001. (Subseries LNAI).

Vol. 2174: F. Baader, G. Brewka, T. Eiter (Eds.), KI 2001: Advances in Artificial Intelligence. Proceedings, 2001. XIII, 471 pages. 2001. (Subseries LNAI).

Vol. 2175: F. Esposito (Ed.), AI*IA 2001: Advances in Artificial Intelligence. Proceedings, 2001. XII, 396 pages. 2001. (Subseries LNAI).

Vol. 2176: K.-D. Althoff, R.L. Feldmann, W. Müller (Eds.), Advances in Learning Software Organizations. Proceedings, 2001. XI, 241 pages. 2001.

Vol. 2177: G. Butler, S. Jarzabek (Eds.), Generative and Component-Based Software Engineering. Proceedings, 2001. X, 203 pages. 2001.

Vol. 2180: J. Welch (Ed.), Distributed Computing. Proceedings, 2001. X, 343 pages. 2001.

Vol. 2181: C. Y. Westort (Ed.), Digital Earth Moving. Proceedings, 2001. XII, 117 pages. 2001.

Vol. 2182: M. Klusch, F. Zambonelli (Eds.), Cooperative Information Agents V. Proceedings, 2001. XII, 288 pages. 2001. (Subseries LNAI).

Vol. 2183: R. Kahle, P. Schroeder-Heister, R. Stärk (Eds.), Proof Theory in Computer Science. Proceedings, 2001. IX, 239 pages. 2001.

Vol. 2184: M. Tucci (Ed.), Multimedia Databases and Image Communication. Proceedings, 2001. X, 225 pages. 2001.

Vol. 2185: M. Gogolla, C. Kobryn (Eds.), «UML» 2001 – The Unified Modeling Language. Proceedings, 2001. XIV, 510 pages. 2001.

Vol. 2186: J. Bosch (Ed.), Generative and Component-Based Software Engineering. Proceedings, 2001. VIII, 177 pages. 2001.

Vol. 2187: U. Voges (Ed.), Computer Safety, Reliability and Security. Proceedings, 2001. XVI, 249 pages. 2001.

Vol. 2188: F. Bomarius, S. Komi-Sirviö (Eds.), Product Focused Software Process Improvement. Proceedings, 2001. XI, 382 pages. 2001.

Vol. 2189: F. Hoffmann, D.J. Hand, N. Adams, D. Fisher, G. Guimaraes (Eds.), Advances in Intelligent Data Analysis. Proceedings, 2001. XII, 384 pages. 2001.

Vol. 2190: A. de Antonio, R. Aylett, D. Ballin (Eds.), Intelligent Virtual Agents. Proceedings, 2001. VIII, 245 pages. 2001. (Subseries LNAI).

Vol. 2191: B. Radig, S. Florczyk (Eds.), Pattern Recognition. Proceedings, 2001. XVI, 452 pages. 2001.

Vol. 2192: A. Yonezawa, S. Matsuoka (Eds.), Metalevel Architectures and Separation of Crosscutting Concerns. Proceedings, 2001. XI, 283 pages. 2001.

Vol. 2193: F. Casati, D. Georgakopoulos, M.-C. Shan (Eds.), Technologies for E-Services. Proceedings, 2001. X, 213 pages. 2001.

Vol. 2194: A.K. Datta, T. Herman (Eds.), Self-Stabilizing Systems. Proceedings, 2001. VII, 229 pages. 2001.

Vol. 2195: H.-Y. Shum, M. Liao, S.-F. Chang (Eds.), Advances in Multimedia Information Processing – PCM 2001. Proceedings, 2001. XX, 1149 pages. 2001.

Vol. 2196: W. Taha (Ed.), Semantics, Applications, and Implementation of Program Generation. Proceedings, 2001. X, 219 pages. 2001.

Vol. 2197: O. Balet, G. Subsol, P. Torguet (Eds.), Virtual Storytelling. Proceedings, 2001. XI, 213 pages. 2001.

Vol. 2198: N. Zhong, Y. Yao, J. Liu, S. Ohsuga (Eds.), Web Intelligence: Research and Development. Proceedings, 2001. XVI, 615 pages. 2001. (Subseries LNAI).

Vol. 2199: J. Crespo, V. Maojo, F. Martin (Eds.), Medical Data Analysis. Proceedings, 2001. X, 311 pages. 2001.

Vol. 2200: G.I. Davida, Y. Frankel (Eds.), Information Security. Proceedings, 2001. XIII, 554 pages. 2001.

Vol. 2201: G.D. Abowd, B. Brumitt, S. Shafer (Eds.), Ubicomp 2001: Ubiquitous Computing. Proceedings, 2001. XIII, 372 pages. 2001.

Vol. 2202: A. Restivo, S. Ronchi Della Rocca, L. Roversi (Eds.), Theoretical Computer Science. Proceedings, 2001. XI, 440 pages. 2001.

Vol. 2204: A. Brandstädt, V.B. Le (Eds.), Graph-Theoretic Concepts in Computer Science. Proceedings, 2001. X, 329 pages. 2001.

Vol. 2205: D.R. Montello (Ed.), Spatial Information Theory. Proceedings, 2001. XIV, 503 pages. 2001.

Vol. 2206: B. Reusch (Ed.), Computational Intelligence. Proceedings, 2001. XVII, 1003 pages. 2001.

Vol. 2207: I.W. Marshall, S. Nettles, N. Wakamiya (Eds.), Active Networks. Proceedings, 2001. IX, 165 pages. 2001.

Vol. 2208: W.J. Niessen, M.A. Viergever (Eds.), Medical Image Computing and Computer-Assisted Intervention – MICCAI 2001. Proceedings, 2001. XXXV, 1446 pages. 2001.

Vol. 2209: W. Jonker (Ed.), Databases in Telecommunications II. Proceedings, 2001. VII, 179 pages. 2001.

Vol. 2210: Y. Liu, K. Tanaka, M. Iwata, T. Higuchi, M. Yasunaga (Eds.), Evolvable Systems: From Biology to Hardware. Proceedings, 2001. XI, 341 pages. 2001.

Vol. 2211: T.A. Henzinger, C.M. Kirsch (Eds.), Embedded Software. Proceedings, 2001. IX, 504 pages. 2001.

Vol. 2212: W. Lee, L. Mé, A. Wespi (Eds.), Recent Advances in Intrusion Detection. Proceedings, 2001. X, 205 pages. 2001.

Vol. 2213: M.J. van Sinderen, L.J.M. Nieuwenhuis (Eds.), Protocols for Multimedia Systems. Proceedings, 2001. XII, 239 pages. 2001.

Vol. 2215: N. Kobayashi, B.C. Pierce (Eds.), Theoretical Aspects of Computer Software. Proceedings, 2001. XV, 561 pages. 2001.

Vol. 2216: E.S. Al-Shaer (Ed.), Management of Multimedia Networks and Services. Proceedings, 2001. XIV, 373 pages. 2001.

Vol. 2217: T. Gomi (Ed.), Evolutionary Robotics. Proceedings, 2001. XI, 139 pages. 2001.

Printed in the United States
By Bookmasters